THE
LITTLE
BOOK
OF
BIRMINGHAM

NORMAN BARTLAM

The
History
Press

First published 2011

The History Press
The Mill, Brimscombe Port
Stroud, Gloucestershire, GL5 2QG
www.thehistorypress.co.uk

British Library Cataloguing in Publication Data.
A catalogue record for this book is available from the British Library.

ISBN 978 0 7524 6349 0

Typesetting and origination by The History Press
Printed in Great Britain

CONTENTS

INTRODUCTION

The *Little Book of Birmingham* is, as the title suggests, a little book, about Birmingham – a little bit about a lot – not a boring gazetteer or a glossy, overproduced promotional guide to the city, but a down-to-earth collection of quirky and interesting facts that will have you saying 'I didn't know I didn't know that!'

I feel sure you will read something here that you will commit to memory and will rush off and tell your friends about. In fact, why not go up to a complete stranger on the no. 11 bus and tell him if he travelled the full circle he'd go past 266 bus stops; then go to Harborne and tell people a man from there once grew the biggest gooseberry ever produced in England; then for good measure tell them that Noele Gordon from *Crossroads* was called Noele because she was born on Christmas Day . . . I guarantee it will be a great way to make new friends.

If these people ignore you, you can always go home and snuggle up in bed with the next chapter of *The Little Book of Birmingham,* safe in the knowledge that you are part of the great city that is Birmingham, even though there are six roads that meet at Five Ways, the site of the last public hanging was marked by a plaque in the wrong place and that a wallaby 'christened' the floor at the opening of the International Convention Centre!

Intrigued? I hope so.

Read on and discover more about the past and present of the 'City of a Thousand Trades', in more than a thousand quirky facts . . . just don't recite them to me on the no. 11 bus!

Norman Bartlam, 2011

WHAT THEY SAID ABOUT BRUM

'The only prosperous people were the publicans. What have people got to do but drink here? It's their only comfort'.

William White report to Parliament in 1867

'A Brummie is anyone born in striking distance of Longbridge'.

Many comedians

'I'm in this immense industrial city where they make excellent knives, scissors, springs, files and goodness knows what else and besides these, music too. And how well! It's terrifying how much these people here manage to achieve.'

Dvořák on a visit to Birmingham, 1880

'Birmingham: the hardware town, where there were ten times as many metal workers as there were builders, ten times as many general tradesmen and craftsmen as professional men.'

Universal British Dictionary

'The whirl of the wheels and noise of machinery shook the trembling walls. The fires whose lurid sullen light had been visible for miles blazed fiercely up on the great works and factories of the town.'

Charles Dickens

'Birmingham, swarming with inhabitants and echoing with the noise of anvils.'

Camden

'One has no great hope of Birmingham. I always say there is something direful in the sound.'

Mrs Elton in *Emma* by Jane Austen

'The Clent Hills offer an escape for pale faced artisans and over laboured clerks broken loose for a few happy days from the din and smoke of the more distant Birmingham.'

Hugh Miller, traveller in *First Impressions of England and Its People*

'A vile, stone clad bruiser; a huge bulge of beige and glass, draped in pretty detail in a ridiculous attempt to hide its hideous size. It's an elephant in a tutu.'

Tom Dyckhoff of *The Times* describes the new Bullring

'There is land for six ploughs.'

The Domesday Book

'We are a city of Philosophers; we work with our heads and make the boobies of Birmingham work with us with their hands.'

Dr Johnson of Lichfield, 1776

'I approached her [Birmingham] with reluctance, because I did not know her; I shall leave her with reluctance, because I do.'

William Hutton, 1781

'Birmingham is the home of the best traditions of municipal life and I am well assured that these traditions will be upheld in the future as they have been in the past.'

King Edward VII, 1909

'Probably in no other age or country was there ever such an astonishing display of human ingenuity as may be found in Birmingham.'

Robert Southey, poet, 1807

1

EARLY DAYS

IN THE BEGINNING

The name Birmingham came from the Anglo-Saxon words 'ham', or homestead, of the family, 'ing', of 'Beorma', or Birm.

Birmingham consisted of just nine families and the household of the Lord of the Manor when the Domesday Book was compiled in 1086.

A DOZEN PLACE NAMES FROM THE DOMESDAY BOOK

Sutone:	Sutton Coldfield
Celboldstone:	Edgbaston
Estone:	Aston
Nordfield:	Northfield
Escelie:	Selly Oak
Nortune:	Kings Norton
Museleie:	Moseley
Gerlei:	Yardley
Pirio:	Perry Barr
Horeborne:	Harborne
Honesworde:	Handsworth
Merstone:	Marston Green

The Bullring is often a disappointment for our Spanish visitors as it is not the place to see bulls being attacked with swords, and never has been. Neither is it a place for particularly good tapas, but that's beside the point. The Bullring was a metal ring in the ground where farmers tethered their bulls at the market.

Peter de Birmingham gained a charter to have a market in Birmingham in 1166. At that time the small settlement was clustered around his moated manor house at the present-day Bullring.

In 1250 William de Birmingham was granted 'de right' to have a four-day fair at 'Ascension tide'.

The 'oldest piece of work done by men's hands in the town' is thought to be the tomb of one of the de Birmingham family members who died in 1306.

The last of the de Birmingham family, Edward, was born in 1497 and was only three when he succeeded his grandfather to the manor of Birmingham.

Edward de Bimingham was arrested over an incident with John Dudley, 1st Duke of Northumberland, and imprisoned in the Tower of London for four years until being pardoned in 1536.

The name Bullring appears as 'LeBulrynge' in a document related to land owned by the King Edward Schools in 1552.

When new building plots were put up for sale on Temple Street in 1743 the accompanying blurb noted they had, 'adjoining fields with a prospect of four miles distant.'

Birmingham-born John Rogers was burned at the stake in London in 1555 after condemning the religious views of the new Queen Mary. A plaque in his honour can be seen in Digbeth.

Northfield still keeps the pound, but it can't be spent in the nearby pub, although it is attached to it. This pound is the one where stray animals were locked up and released when the owner paid a suitable fine and it has been there for over 500 years.

Anne Boleyn, the queen who lost her head over Henry VIII, was a notable parishioner of St Leonard's Church at Frankley.

The stump of the Selly Oak tree was placed in the nearby park after being felled by a fella, or maybe tree fellas, in 1909 at the junction where the main roads met in Selly Oak. This is the tree from which the name of the suburb derives.

Bartley Green is also linked to the local flora and fauna. It was known as Berchelai Whein, which means a clearing of birch trees.

In the autumn of 1642, with the outbreak of Civil War between Parliament and King Charles I, the first great clash took place at Edgehill, around 30 miles from Brum. The king passed through Birmingham and addressed his troops. The place where he stopped off became known as Kingstanding, which somehow sounds better than Kingsittingdown. It has, however, been suggested that a 'Standing' was another name for a hunting lodge but that doesn't make such a good story!

Many people assume that Alum Rock is so called because a local company, Southall's, dug artesian wells beneath their premises and came across a layer of rock, a whitish mineral salt which was known as Alum Rock. Historian Carl Chinn points out that the name of the area actually dates back to at least 1760, many years before Southall's were established. So who knows?

Bishop Vesey, even though he's been dead since the sixteenth century, has the honour of having a council ward (Sutton Vesey) named after him – probably the only ward ever to be named after a person. He'd obviously made an impact on the area; he was after all responsible for the town of Sutton becoming a royal town and for one of the largest parks in Europe.

Kitwell near Bartley Green is named after a small well. The waters contained iron which was supposed to have health-giving properties, although it wasn't too healthy for a lad called Christopher, or Kit for short, for he fell in and drowned – but at least he had the place of his death named after him!

Nearby is the area of California named by Issac Flavel when he returned from the California gold rush in the 1840s. The stones he found here were not gold but were used to manufacture bricks. An earlier brickworks in the locality was set up by John Barnes, hence Barnes Hill, and the famous local youth club is called the Stonehouse Gang.

Sarehole Mill, a restored eighteenth-century water-powered cornmill at Hall Green is a direct link with Birmingham's past. The current building was rebuilt in the 1760s and was in use commercially until 1919.

Birmingham does have its own castle, Weoley Castle, built in the twelfth or thirteenth century. It was officially a fortified moated manor house that dates back to 1264. It was in the hands of the de Somery family and later the Jervoises. Daniel Ledsam bought it in 1809 and Birmingham City Council purchased it in 1930. However, it deteriorated to such an extent that it was closed to the public in 1996. Well done Birmingham City Council!

Birmingham does have another castle; it's the *Clun Castle*, a steam locomotive named after the Shropshire town.

The Artisans Dwellings Act of 1875 gave local authorities the power to buy and redevelop areas of land. A new street was subsequently cut through a slum area in the town centre and 16,000 people were displaced. Roads such as The Gullet were demolished. The new road was 22 yards wide and resembled, at that time at least, a Parisian boulevard. As this road was a magnificent thoroughfare designed by the Corporation, it became known as Corporation Street.

In July 1938 two dinosaurs were spotted roaming around Aston Park; they were part of the historical recreation of the centenary of Birmingham being granted a charter of incorporation in 1838. The pageant in the park included numerous floats and exhibitions.

SIX MILLS A-WHIRLING

Thimble Mill on Aston Brook, Nechells.
Sarehole Mill near the River Cole.
Heath Mill on the River Rea.
Duddeston Mill on the River Rea.
Pebble Mill was on the Bournbrook.
Titterford Mill on the River Cole.

SIX OFFICERS OF THE COURT LEET

The Court Leet was a council of the free men of the Manor.

The High Bailiff. He saw order was kept at markets and fairs and that weights and measures were true.

The Low Bailiff. He had to summon the jury.

The Constable or Headborough. He had similar duties to the constables of today.

The Ale Connors or High Tasters. They had to check beer tasted good – a nasty job, but someone had to do it.

The Fish Connors or Low Tasters. They checked to see if food offered for sale was good.

Searchers and sealers of leather. They examined leather to check it was tanned.

BIRMINGHAM'S THIRTEEN ANCIENT MONUMENTS

Sutton Park

Woodlands Park Prehistoric Burnt Mounds

Fox Hollies Prehistoric Burnt Mounds

Moseley Bog Prehistoric Burnt Mounds

Peddimore Hall

Kent's Moat

Gannow Green Moat

Birmingham's Roman Fort, Metchley

Hawkesley Farm Moat

Kingstanding Mound

Weoley Castle

Perry Bridge

Gullitone Lock

2

LONGEST, TALLEST & OLDEST

THE TEN TALLEST STRUCTURES IN BIRMINGHAM

Sutton Coldfield TV transmitter, 1959, 245 metres, 804ft

BT Tower, 1966, 152 metres, 498ft high

Radisson Hotel, Holloway Circus, 2005, 130 metres, 427ft

Alpha Tower, 1973, 100 metres, 328ft, over 28 floors

Joseph Chamberlain Clock, Birmingham University, 1909, 100 metres, 328ft

Orion Office and residential block, 2007, 90 metres, 295ft

Clydesale Tower residential block, Holloway Head, 1972, 90 metres, 295ft

Cleveland Tower residential block, Holloway Head, 1972, 90 metres, 295ft

The Rotunda office block now residential, 1965, 81 metres, 266ft

103 Colmore Row former Nat West office block, 1976, 80 metres, 262ft

HIGHEST POINTS

The highest point in the city is the roadway around Quinton High Street at 736ft above sea level. You can aspire to a higher view, but sitting on top of Quinton parish church spire would be a rather uncomfortable place to position yourself.

The Lickey Hills reach 956ft above sea level, and Barr Beacon is 744ft, but they are technically over the Brummie border.

The other high points are Frankley at 604ft, Kings Norton old golf course at 550ft, Great Barr at 500ft and Victoria Square in the city centre is 450ft above sea level.

It is said that the next highest point from Quinton High Street in an easterly direction is to be found overseas in the Ural Mountains, or as locals have been known to say, 'Next highest place from here is the urinals.'

As any discerning football fan will know, The Hawthorns, home to West Bromwich Albion, is the place where football is played at the highest level. At 550ft above sea level, the stadium is the highest professional football ground in the country.

THE LARGEST & SMALLEST

Birmingham City Council is the largest local authority in the UK and the largest council in Europe with 120 councillors representing 40 wards.

The city's largest single-day event is its St Patrick's Day parade. Indeed, it is Europe's second largest, after the one in Dublin.

By 1889, the Birmingham Mint had become the largest private mint in the world, and was the oldest continuously operating mint.

Sutton Park is one of the largest urban parks in Europe, and is the largest outside a capital city, at 24,000 acres.

When it was built in 1916 the tyre store, which became known as Fort Dunlop, was the largest concrete and steel erection in Europe and at one time it was the world's largest factory, employing 3,200 workers.

The largest peace pagoda in Europe, the Dhamma Talaka Pagoda in Osler Street, opened in 1998. It was topped with a 60ft-high golden dome guarded by two lions, and it is modelled on the Shwedagon Pagoda in Yangon (formerly Rangoon) in Myanmar. The dome was described in the local press as looking like 'a caramel flavoured Angel Delight or a 99 ice cream without the chocolate flake'.

In 1930, Birmingham Corporation had a fleet of 843 trams, the largest of any city in the world.

The IMAX Cinema at Millennium Point has the largest screen in the Midlands. It is 22 metres wide and 16 metres high. IMAX says it is as tall as a five-storey building and as wide as four buses parked nose to tail.

The largest Sikh temple in Europe was built in 1991 on Soho Road, Handsworth. Its 100ft high dome certainly stands out.

When it was first mooted that it was about to be sold in 1997, the Royal Mail sorting office in central Birmingham was the largest of its type in Europe, with around 1,000 employees processing over three million items per day.

Daniel Lambert, 1770–1809, was the largest man in the country. For a while he worked as an apprentice at an engraving and die casting works in Birmingham. At the time of his death he weighed 52 stone 11lb, and his coffin required 112sq ft of wood.

St Philip's Cathedral in Colmore Row is the third smallest cathedral in the country, at 13,720sq ft with seating for around 1,000 people. It was built in 1715 as a parish church and did not become a cathedral until 1905. I bet like me you're keen to know the two cathedrals that are smaller than Brum's? Well, right on pew here's the answer. Derby and Chelmsford cathedrals are both smaller than St Philip's.

The Prince of Wales visited Birmingham in November 1926 and at the Livestock Show at Bingley Hall he saw a huge 68lb cabbage, which was probably a record size and never eaten or beaten again.

The Frankfurt Christmas Market, held annually since 2001 has become the UK's largest outdoor Christmas market, and the largest German market outside of Germany itself. Last year it attracted 3.1 million visitors.

Birmingham-born microsculptor Willard Wigan creates microscopic works of art, using some of the tiniest but strongest materials known to man, from nylon, gold, one grain of sand, human hair to the shortest eyelash. In recognition of his service to the arts, Wigan received an MBE in 2007. No doubt it was a full-sized one!

In 1875 a member of the Harborne Gooseberry Growers' Association made headline news when he grew the largest gooseberry in England. The gooseberry in question weighed in at 1½ ounces and was apparently called Bobby. The gooseberry wasn't preserved but the scales were – they are said to be in the collection of Birmingham Museum & Art Gallery.

THE LONG, THE TALL & SHORT OF IT

The longest-serving driver with Birmingham Corporation Tramways Department, Frank Bissell, was in charge of the last tram in Birmingham on 4 July 1953. Tram no. 616 left the depot for the final time with the lord mayor among the passengers.

The Lapal canal tunnel was the fourth longest in the country but a roof fall 20 yards from the Halesowen end closed it in 1917.

This isn't a tall story, it's true: Birmingham's City's Serbian striker Nikola Zigic, 30, was the tallest player in the Premierhip until Brum's relegation in 2010/11, standing at 6ft 8in. Stoke City's Peter Crouch is only 6ft 7in tall.

The shortest street name in Birmingham is AB Row, so called because it was at the boundary of the parishes of Aston and Birmingham.

In early 2011 the city council built Birmingham's shortest bicycle lane on Watford Road, Cotteridge, it stops almost as soon as it has started because it is less than 15 metres long! A bicycle spokesman said it was 'pathetic'.

OLDEST & YOUNGEST

The oldest rocks found in Birmingham are located in the south-west near Rednal where there is what is officially described as 'unfossiliferous quartzites of Lower Cambrian age'.

The Electric Cinema, opened on 27 December 1909, is the UK's oldest working cinema. It was Birmingham's first cinema and predated the introduction of the 1909 Cinematograph Act that commenced in January 1910.

Birmingham's longest established business Firmin & Sons Ltd in New Town Row, which manufactures badges and buttons, was thought to have been established by 1677, but recent research has uncovered a document showing the firm was in business in 1655, so the oldest business is even older than we thought.

In 1997 Karren Brady, at Birmingham City FC, became the youngest managing director of a UK plc.

Curzon Street station, which closed to trains in 1966, is said to be the world's oldest surviving piece of railway architecture.

The Lad in the Lane pub has been recognised as Birmingham's oldest house, once known as the Old Green Man. The pub has a long history with some beams dating back to 1306. Dendrochronology has verified the age of the pub, thanks to local historian Peter Leather and his team. The Old Crown, dating back to 1386, was until recently said to be the oldest pub in Birmingham as well as the oldest example of a timber-framed house still standing in the city.

The world's oldest press club can be traced back to 1865 when a small group of journalists met at a hotel in the centre of Birmingham. The original minutes book records, 'meeting, held for the purpose of establishing a Club for promoting social enjoyment and literary recreation among Reporters and others connected with the Newspaper Press of Birmingham, held at Suffield's Hotel, Union Passage, on Saturday, the 16th of December, 1865.' Among its first rules was the edict that the reporters connected with the *Daily Post*, the *Daily Gazette* and the *Midland Counties Herald* should be its first members.

In October 2010 when Susannah Rudge became curate at St Francis', Bournville's parish church, she became the youngest person to enter the priesthood in the Church of England Diocese of Birmingham. She was twenty-six.

Birmingham is the youngest city in Europe with a higher proportion of people aged under fifteen than any other city in the European Union, with 37 per cent of the population aged under twenty-five.

3

EVENTS & HAPPENINGS

TEN ROYAL VISITS

On 7 July 1909 King Edward VII and Queen Alexandra visited the city to open Birmingham University. Shops and factories shut and thousands of people lined the streets. Industrial concerns showed off their wares in the form of triumphal arches. The arches were:

The School of Art's turreted gates decorated with the coat of arms
Water Department Arch on Broad Street outside the Water
    Department offices, showing off the success of the Elan Valley
    water supply system
Fireman's Arch
Gas Department's Arch
Cycle Manufacturers' Arch
Metallic Bedstead Makers' Arch

In March 1887 Queen Victoria visited Birmingham to lay the foundation stone for the Victoria Law Courts on Corporation Street. This was in fact the day before her birthday and was her golden jubilee year.

In July 1915 King George visited the city and toured factories involved in the war effort, including BSA, where he is said to have been interested in the firing of the Automatic Lewis guns.

The Duke of York, later to become King George VI, officially opened Aston Villa's magnificent red-brick main stand on Trinity Road in 1924. He said that he had no idea that a ground so finely equipped in every way and devoted to football existed. Shame they demolished it recent years!

The New Inns pub at Handsworth is the only pub in the country to have received a royal opening. The Prince of Wales, later Edward VII, opened a bar, thoughtfully named the Prince's Suite, in 1932. The pub has since been converted into flats, which may, or may not, be haunted by spirits.

The Prince of Wales visited The Hawthorns, home of WBA, on 11 May 1931 'when he congratulated the players and officials on the achievement of winning the Football Association Cup and promotion to Division 1 of the Football League in the same season 1930–1931'.

The Queen Mother opened the hospital named in her honour in March 1939. She was due to attend the official opening in summer 1938, but the Duke of Gloucester deputised for the royal couple. The first patients were accepted in December 1938 before the Queen Mother's official unveiling.

On 30 April 1988 the Queen Mother opened the redevelopment of the Botanical Gardens by planting a commemorative tree, using the shiniest spade ever seen! The tree was a Betula costata.

The newly revamped Victoria Square was officially opened by Diana, Princess of Wales, on 6 May 1993.

Princess Anne officially opened BBC Birmingham's new broadcasting centre in The Mailbox on 9 September 2004. She also opened the BBC's former site at Pebble Mill in 1971.

CRIMINAL EVENTS

The Priestley Riots took place from 14 to 17 July 1791 during which attacks were made on religious dissenters including Joseph Priestley. The riots started with an attack on a hotel that was the site of a banquet organised in sympathy with the French Revolution. Then, beginning with Priestley's church and home, the rioters attacked or burned four dissenting chapels, twenty-seven houses and several businesses.

In 1901, David Lloyd George, an outspoken supporter of the Boer cause in the South African War, spoke at the Town Hall. The majority of people in Birmingham were, however, strongly anti-Boer, and the visit caused some ill feeling – well, a little more than some ill feeling actually. The Town Hall was stoned by a baying mob and Lloyd George escaped from the building dressed in a policeman's uniform. He was marched out of the area and smuggled into Ladywood police station.

One of the earliest reports of a fine comes from a record of 1428 when the Jouettes family of Selly Manor were fined twopence over reports that trees were blocking their lane.

'ELLO, 'ELLO, 'ELLO, WHAT'S ALL THIS THEN?

The first police station was established in 1839 with the setting up of the Birmingham Borough Police. The police advertised for 'young men not over 36 years of age or under 5' 8", able to read, write and produce testimonials of exceptional character.' The first recruit was George Howick, twenty-six, who joined up on 23 September 1839.

Birmingham got its first two policewomen on the beat in 1917. Rebecca Lipscombe and Evelyn Miles were lock matrons.

1839 was the year in which the first horse patrols appeared.

The first police motorcycle roared into action in 1921.

Two-way radios were introduced on 5 October 1964 when constables at Coventry Road police station alpha-foxtrotted onto the streets.

On 10 October 1966 Belgrave Road police station took delivery of the force's first three Austin A40 patrol cars.

Today West Midlands Police is the second largest in the country, covering an area of 348 square miles and serving a population of nearly 2.6 million.

The police helicopter flew 3,315 times in 2008–9. It flies at a speed which means two miles of ground can be covered in one minute's flying time.

TWENTY WAYS TO APPEAR BEFORE BIRMINGHAM POLICE COURT

Alfred Hudson, 'a young scamp resident' of Tower Street, Aston, 'exposed his person in a disgusting manner at the window of Mr. Chaplin's shop in Bull Street'. He repeated the offence on three occasions and on 3 December 1857 the Bench 'ordered the low fellow to be imprisoned for three months with hard labour'.

A youth named Richard Reynolds, a tinplate worker of Moor Street, was charged with stealing a silk scarf. He said he was ill at the time he stole from his lodger and that he really wanted bread. On 15 December 1857 he was sentenced to one day's imprisonment.

Thomas Goodwin, reckless looking youth and by trade a shoemaker, was charged with wilfully breaking a window of the Parish Offices in Paradise Street because he had been refused a ticket of relief. In April 1858 he was ordered to pay 5s damages and costs; in default fourteen days' hard labour.

'A good looking girl' named Martha Dunn was seen, at 3.00 a.m. in Church Street, 'making a great noise and uttering the most obscene language'. In court in April 1858, she was dressed in 'the garb of ultra-finery, and looking a picture to a slave of abandoned habits, the wretched young creature had nothing to say.' The press noted, 'Mr. Kynnersley hardly knew what to do in such a sad case, but ultimately sent her to gaol for seven days'.

On 24 June 1861, a young man named William Horn, of King Edwards Road, a bedstead caster, was brought up by PC Spiers, charged with playing with a lot of boys at the game of pitch and toss in Cope Street. The offence was proved, but the mother of the accused begged for a lenient fine, as her son was her main support. After a suitable caution, the youth was fined 2s 6d, without any costs.

In August 1864, William Biddle, lapidary, Well Street, was charged with stealing three ducks belonging to Mr Bird. He and two others were seen by a police officer walking with the ducks under their arms, which they threw down as they ran up an entry when spotted. Biddle said he 'was out for a walk'. He was ordered to be imprisoned for six weeks.

William Clarence, aged fourteen, of Blews Street, was sentenced to twenty-one days' imprisonment for stealing a number of apples from a garden on Birmingham Heath in October 1866.

A young woman, giving the name Fanny Harris, a domestic servant of Moseley Street, was charged with stealing two spoons, the property of Mrs Holmes of Cherry Street. Mrs Holmes saw the prisoner 'in the act of decamping down the cellar steps' and she saw the spoons on the steps. The prisoner said she had gone to visit her, and as she was her former mistress, 'upon hearing something, which she thought was the dog approaching her, she was frightened and ran down into the cellar.' The magistrate gave her the benefit of the doubt and discharged her.

In November 1867, Fred Davis, aged eleven, of Adelaide Street, was charged with stealing a jug and glass, the property of his mother. The prisoner was said to be 'a very bad lad' and his mother could do nothing with him. He was sentenced to fourteen days' imprisonment and afterwards to be sent to Penn Street Industrial School for five years.

Four men were charged in June 1869 with stealing a tub of butter, valued at 2*s* 8*d*. A quantity of butter was being transported from Birmingham to West Bromwich when it was discovered that 'a 48lb tub had been stolen from the wagon'. It was found in the home of one of the villains, who was described as 'a clever thief'; he was sentenced to six months and the other two to four months each (no doubt news of the butter theft quickly 'spread' around the neighbourhood).

Thomas Morgan, 'a strongly built man', was charged with assault in a beer house in Rea Street. He struck two men 'with violent blows upon the head with handle of a fire shovel'. A police constable who was called in said the taproom of the beer house was 'like a slaughterhouse, and nearly everyone there was bleeding'. He was committed for two months for each assault in January 1870.

William Thompson appeared in court on 7 October 1870 charged with stealing a woman's purse by cutting at her pocket in the Market Hall. He was said to be 'imperfectly educated', but was sentenced to six months' imprisonment.

Thomas White, seventeen, a brass caster of Bagot Street, was charged with stealing seven dozen sticks of rhubarb and some potatoes from a shed near the canal on Bagot Street. He appeared before the court on 3 July 1871 and was committed for fourteen days.

Thomas Miller, twelve, of Icknield Port Road, was charged with stealing a live lark from a stall in the Market Hall. A police office searched the prisoner and found 'the lark with its legs broken, in one of the pockets of his trousers'. The prisoner was remanded in November 1871.

Ginovario Curio, aged seventeen, appeared in court on 18 February 1873 where he was described as 'an itinerant musician'. He was charged with assaulting Lewis Thompson of Great Tindal Street. 'It appeared some boys interfered with him whilst he was playing a harp on Waterloo Street'. Curio attacked one of the boys involved 'in a violent manner'. He was fined 5s with costs. 'The defendant's harp was produced in court, and was a little damaged'.

Thirty-five-year-old labourer James Clutterbuck of Springfield Street appeared before the court in March 1873, charged with stealing two iron pig troughs from a premises in Smethwick. The prisoner eventually pleaded guilty and was sentenced to twenty-one days' imprisonment. No doubt he was disgruntled.

Thomas Harborne, aged fifteen, appeared in court on 3 March 1874, and was fined 5s plus costs for throwing stones with other youths in Portland Road. 'One of the stones struck a man and knocked a hole in his hat'.

David Buckell of Moseley Road was charged with 'unlawfully leaving a train whilst in motion, contrary to the laws of the London & North Western Railway Company'. As a train pulled into New Street station, Buckell 'alighted from the train, fell forward and rolled on to the platform, his legs coming into contact with carriages of the train'. He 'attempted to justify his conduct by stating that the train ought not to have gone so far up the platform'. In May 1876 he was fined 2s plus costs, or in default, fourteen days' imprisonment.

Joseph Cook, a fishmonger of Great Lister Street, appeared in court in November 1876 and was summoned with 'having exposed for sale 337 pilchards which were unfit for human food'. He claimed that he was not going to sell the fish and was keeping them in his shop until the arrival of the dustcart. He was fined 5s and costs, amounting together 18s.

In March 1893 William Matthews, aged forty-five, a gardener, was charged with willfully damaging a quantity of growing plants at Summerfield Park. A gardener saw the prisoner pulling up some pinks and violas and was wrapping them up when he was caught. The prisoner said the plants were his own. The Bench said that they had not the slightest doubt that the prisoner had taken the plants and it was a very bad case. The Corporation provided a beautiful park for the use of the public. He had to pay 2*s* damages, and a fine of 20*s* and costs or, in default, would have to go to gaol for one month, with hard labour.

I'M DYING TO TELL YOU ABOUT . . .

The three men depicted on Broad Street's golden statue, pioneers of the industrial revolution, Boulton, Watt and Murdoch, are all buried in the same churchyard, St Mary's in Handsworth. The same cemetery is home to the remains of William McGregor who organised the meeting that set up the Football League in 1888, and George Ramsay, one of the founders of Aston Villa.

The Office of National Statistics produced a report in 2008 that showed that men in Sutton Four Oaks Ward could expect to live 2.4 years longer than the national average of 76 years. The figure for women was 1.2 years above national average of 80.5 years.

John Howes survived the Charge of the Light Brigade, one of the country's great military disasters, but passed away on Christmas Day 1902 at his home in Spring Road, Edgbaston, and is now buried in Lodge Hill cemetery.

A gravestone in Edgbaston Old Church has a foxglove engraved on it. This is in memory of Dr William Withering who died in 1799, after discovering the curative properties of digitalis, an extract of foxglove.

A memorial to John Heap and William Badger in the form of part of a column from the Town Hall stands in St Philip's churchyard. They were killed when scaffolding collapsed on them while the building was being erected in 1883. For a number of years the Trades Union Congress held an annual service at the memorial.

At Elmdon church there are two animal-related headstones. One is for Josephine the Cat and the other Rehoboam, a cockerel. Josephine's gravestone reads: 'The faithful friend and constant companion of the late W C Alston at Elmdon Hall September 28 1920 much missed by his owner Mrs. Kent'. Rehoboam was 'my silky cockerel died 31 December 1919, deeply lamented'.

The year 1665 is thought of as the year of the Great Plague, but the register of St Martin's in the Bullring doesn't record any extraordinary mortality figures. Likewise the area of Ladywood was noted on maps as being the 'Pest grounds' but again there seems to be little evidence of a huge number of burials.

St Peter's Church on Broad Street was demolished in 1969 and today the International Convention Centre occupies the site. Much of the land was scooped out to enable a walkway to be built down to the canalside. Anyone walking along it will be unaware that are walking through what was once the graveyard. The human remains in the graveyard were dug up and reinterred at Oscott cemetery. Official records indicated there were 577 bodies to be found but 1,163 were discovered. The additional remains were thought to have been buried quickly because of a rapidly spreading disease. Some suggest it may have been the plague or cholera that caused the deaths.

In July 1863 an acrobat called 'the female Blondin' was killed when she fell from a tightrope at an event in Aston Park. Her real name was Selina Powell (née Hunt). Queen Victoria was not amused by the incident as she had opened the park to the public five years earlier. She wrote of her dismay 'that one of her subjects, a female, should have been sacrificed to the gratification of the demoralising taste for exhibitions attended with the greatest danger to the performers.'

The former Newman Bros coffin works is being turned into a museum. It made coffin fittings for Princess Diana's coffin and caskets for the funeral of Winston Churchill and Neville Chamberlain were also made there. At one time over 100 people worked at the Fleet Street premises. Shrouds currently on display are even designed in colours of local football teams, although no self-respecting Blues fan would be seen dead in a Villa shroud, or vice versa.

The only fatal casualty resulting from enemy air raids during the First World War was a monkey called Jacko who belonged to Dame Elizabeth Cadbury. Jacko apparently died of fright as bombs were dropped on the Austin car works around a mile or so away from where he lived at Manor House in Northfield.

101 GREAT FUNERALS*

50,000 people lined the route of the funeral cortège of political figure, John Skirrow Wright (1822–89) from the People's Chapel in Great King Street to Key Hill Cemetery.

At the funeral of George Dixon MP in January 1898, thousands of people lined the route from St Augustine's Church to his burial place at Witton Cemetery.

Around 12,000 people attended the funeral procession of anti-slavery campaigner Joseph Sturge in 1859.

A huge crowd of people turned out for the funeral of brewer William Butler to watch the cortège pass from his house at Elmdon to Key Hill Cemetery. The press noted it brought about: 'the greatest concourse of people in Birmingham ever known under like circumstances, and it was estimated that ten thousand persons visited the Cemetery the day after to mark their respect and to view the hundreds of floral tributes sent by sorrowing relatives and friends as a mark of their deep condolence.'

In August 1890, 15,000 mourners lined the funeral route from the Oratory Church in Edgbaston to Cardinal Newman's last resting place at the Oratory Retreat in Rednal.

* Maybe not quite 101.

Well-known politician Joseph Chamberlain is buried alongside Harriet Chamberlain, his first wife, Florence Chamberlain, his second wife and an infant son. His family declined a burial in Westminster Abbey and opted for a Unitarian burial in Birmingham. On 5 July 1914 his body was sent on a train from Paddington to Birmingham. The next day he was buried in the family plot at Key Hill Cemetery.

Matthew Boulton's funeral was held in August 1809 with around 700 official mourners. The cortège consisted of 22 carriages and a procession of 500 men and 50 women who wished to pay their respects to the man who helped to make Birmingham 'the workshop of the world'.

Lord Herbert Austin of motor car fame died on 23 May 1941, after a short illness at the age of seventy-four, and is buried in Holy Trinity Church, Rose Hill, North Worcestershire (usually called the Lickey Church). It is said that he attended the funeral of workers killed in a bombing raid at the Longbridge factory in November 1940, and he caught a chill from which he never fully recovered.

Chief Superintendent Alfred Tozer of the Birmingham Fire Brigade was buried on 28 April 1906. Supt Tozer, whose father and grandfather had been firemen before him, came to Birmingham in 1879 and was instrumental in developing a modern fire brigade for the city. The funeral took place at St Bartholomew's, the parish church of Edgbaston. Some of the mourners were veterans of the Crimean War that had taken place fifty years earlier, and this presumably relates to the fact that Supt Tozer's father had overseen the fire arrangements at the Scutari and other Crimean War hospitals.

WINSON GREEN PRISON

The first cell door creaked open on 17 October 1849 and quickly closed on the occupant. The first prison was opened in Peck Lane, just off New Street, in the 1730s, and a later prison existed on Moor Street before Winson Green was built.

It cost around £60,000 to build and had 336 cells, which almost doubled to 612 by 1885.

The first governor was Captain Alexander Maconochie and he fought for penal reform arguing, 'that cruelty debases both victim and the society inflicting it, and that punishment for crime should not be vindictive but designed to strengthen a prisoner's desire and capacity to observe social constraints.' He was dismissed after complaints of lack of discipline within the prison. He was criticised for his actions, in spite of being praised for his humanity and benevolence.

Maconochie's replacement, Lieutenant Austin, was imprisoned for three months after a Home Office Commission confirmed complaints of brutality. The controversy had begun with the suicide of a young inmate in April 1853. Edward Andrews had been committed to Winson Green for two months' hard labour for stealing beef. Although only fifteen years old, this was his third spell inside, the other two for throwing stones in the street and for stealing fruit from a garden. It was the hard labour and the way it was exacted that caused the scandal and caused numerous suicide attempts.

Charlie Wilson, one of the Great Train Robbers, was sentenced to thirty years in the prison, but on 12 August 1964 he escaped just four months into his sentence. Three accomplices are thought to have taken a ladder from a nearby builders' yard to break into the grounds of a hospital next to the prison, and then used a rope ladder to scale the 20ft high prison wall. They coshed one of the two patrolling warders on duty and tied him up before opening Wilson's cell door and freeing him. It is still not known how they got hold of the keys to Wilson's cell. He was recaptured in Canada in January 1968 and was released from prison ten years later, but was shot dead at his villa in Marbella, Spain, in 1990.

Today the prison serves the Crown and Magistrates Courts of Birmingham, Stafford and Wolverhampton and the Magistrates Courts of Burton, Cannock, Lichfield, Rugeley, Sutton Coldfield and Tamworth.

There were 41 inmates who met a grisly end at the gallows between 1885 and 1962.

The first to be hanged was Henry Kimberley on 17 March 1885. He had shot dead a woman in a pub on Paradise Street. Hardly paradise!

The last person to be executed there was twenty-year-old Oswald Grey who was executed on 20 November 1962 for the murder of Thomas Bates in Lee Bank.

Christopher Simcox, a double murderer, was scheduled for execution at the prison on 17 March 1964, but was reprieved.

Dorothea Waddingham was the only woman to be hanged at Winson Green, being so by Tom and Albert Pierrepoint on 16 April 1936. Thirty-six-year-old 'nurse' Waddingham, as she called herself, used morphine to poison one of her elderly patients, eighty-nine-year-old Mrs Louisa Baguley and her disabled daughter, Ada, the motive being gain. 10,000 people congregated outside the gaol on the execution day chanting, 'Stop this mother murder!'

One of the most notorious criminals to be hanged in Winson Green was ex-policeman James Joseph Power, after he was convicted of committing a murder within eyesight of the gaol. He was hanged in 1928. It turned out Power had been discharged from the police service five years previously for assaulting a maid while he was on duty.

FIRE, FIRE, POUR ON WATER!

Up until 1873 fires were dealt with by private insurance companies but in that year they were persuaded to give up their equipment to the town and Birmingham's Fire Brigade unit was formed with five engines, sixteen hoses and thirteen sets of uniforms.

A municipal fire service began in 1874; previously insurance companies dealt with fires.

The earliest record of fire appears to be what was described in 1313 as 'the big fire of the town of Birmingham'.

During the Civil War Birmingham was attacked by Prince Rupert and 87 houses were burnt.

In 1682 the churchwarden at St Martin's in the Bullring purchased twenty leather buckets for use in case of fire.

The first parish fire engine came into use in 1695 under the charge of the aptly named William Burn.

On 6 January 1820 the Theatre Royal in New Street was destroyed by fire and two insurance companies, the Norwich Union and the Birmingham Fire Office, both claimed their engine had been first on the scene.

On 26 August 1878 there was a major fire at a sweet shop in Digbeth. The escape ladder was unusable and the shop owner threw her baby, but the jumping sheets were trampled by a large crowd of onlookers, and the baby later died. She herself jumped to her death.

In February 1878 a matchmaking factory in Ladywood was destroyed by fire. The extent of the damage was said to have been 'considerable' and 'vast quantities' of inflammable materials, boxes and matches were destroyed.

When a flourmill was destroyed by fire in 1878 it aroused a great deal of interest because it is believed that this was the first time the fire brigade had been able to use their new steam engine. The *Birmingham Daily Mail* reported: 'the entire stock, consisting of flour and wheat, to the value of several thousand pounds was destroyed. The steam engine played with capital effect, and had the engine been in attendance at an earlier period of the conflagration, very considerable damage would have undoubtedly have been averted.'

In January 1879 fire ripped through the Library, staff tried in vain to put out the fire using buckets of water. The fire engine arrived forty minutes after the alarm was given due to the absence of a driver! Only 1,000 of the 50,000 volumes were saved. The damage was estimated at £35,000 and it was the 'greatest calamity that has ever befallen

the borough'. The replacement library opened in 1882 and by 1960 it was home to 750,000 volumes. It was demolished in 1974 and the replacement to that is now also due to be destroyed.

In March 1906 'The Great Fire of Jamaica Row' in the Bullring caused damage amounting to around £30,000 when wind whipped up the flames in a hardware store. Part of the fire brigade was already dealing with another fire in Camden Street at the time. Hundreds of onlookers appeared at the scene and ended up with their own souvenir as an artist's impression of the conflagration was produced as a postcard.

A huge explosion and fire ripped through Saltley Gas Works in October 1904. The gasholders were 'among the largest of their kind in the world' capable of holding 6,250,000cu ft of gas. Rumour had it that was caused by a worker lighting a cigarette. It is said that the explosion broke windows within a half mile radius of the site.

Hamstead Colliery was the scene of a disaster in March 1908. It is thought a miner dropped a lighted candle into a box of candles and this set fire to the wooden pit props. 8,000 onlookers appeared at the scene as rescuers got to work. They found the remains of 25 men and 30 pit ponies. The *Birmingham Daily Mail* opened a Relief Fund for bereaved families.

A huge fire gutted the Halford's factory in March 1955 even though it was directly opposite the Central fire station.

A 2003 fire estimated as having caused £15 million of damage destroyed most of the National Motorcycle Museum at Bickenhall – 250 of the 900 exhibits were saved. Geoff Duke, a former motorcycling champion, had opened it in 1984.

In January 1984 fire destroyed Bingley Hall on Broad Street. It is thought the fire began in a tent, an exhibit at the Midlands Caravan, Camping & Leisure Exhibition. At its peak more than 100 firemen using 20 pumps and four hydraulic lifting platforms fought the flames.

WEATHERING THE STORM

Generally Birmingham's winters are mild with temperatures hovering between 3.9°C to 6.9°C and summer temperatures average out at between 15°C and 17°C. The south-west of Birmingham around Northfield and the Lickey Hills gets most rain, typically 55 to 88cm per year with the north-east generally below 55cm. This variation is due to the prevailing rain-bearing winds mainly coming from the south-west.

A month's rain fell in two hours during a freak storm on 15 July 1982. During one 15-minute spell 1½in of rain fell.

Over the wet weekend of 11/12 November 1894 Aston Villa's game against Sheffield United went ahead in torrential rain. It was reported that 'three or four' United players left the field soaked through and refused to play on. The game was completed without the wet blankets and it began raining goals with Villa winning 5–0.

On St Swithin's Day in 1920 (or was it 1923?) areas of Birmingham were hit by a sudden deluge that caused widespread flooding. The Hockley Brook area suffered most with a row of four houses being washed away causing a tidal wave that swept through the suburb. A total of fifty people needed to be rescued from nearby properties. A police officer was awarded five guineas and given three merit stripes for his work.

During a storm in June 1875 a woman in Deritend and fourteen sheep in Small Heath were killed by lightning.

Denis Howell MP for Birmingham, Small Heath, gained notoriety when he was appointed Minister for Drought during the prolonged dry spell that occurred in the summer of 1976. It soon precipitated and the rainmaker tag was to follow him for the rest of his career.

Birmingham held its first Super Prix in 1986, and it was almost wrecked by the tail end of Hurricane Charley that lashed the city with torrential rain and high winds.

In August 1889 there was a heavy and destructive thunderstorm over Birmingham. The press reported one man 'was in the act of raising a knife to his mouth when a flash of lightning passed along the blade and severely burned his cheek. He was informed that the sight of one of his eyes maybe affected. A girl living in Brookfields was wheeling a perambulator down the thoroughfare in which she lived, when she was struck by lightning. 'The current seems to have passed from her head down the left side of her body, tearing her clothing. Singular to say, the lightning cut the crown clean from her hat, leaving the rim intact. Her face was charred, and the hair singed off her head.'

In 1930 the Great Carmo Circus Menagerie and Horse Show suffered from the heavy snow. The huge tent capable of accommodating 4,000 people sitting and 1,000 standing, collapsed under the weight of more than 100 tons of snow.

Today a few millimetres of snow brings the city to a standstill, but that wasn't always the case. Heavy snow was just an irritation that had to be overcome. During the great snowfall of January 1940 it was estimated 7,000,000 tons of snow fell on Birmingham, damaging 7,000 homes. 16in of snow fell, the largest amount since 1895.

In January 1947 Birmingham received heavy snow and temperatures of -20°C.

On 14 January 1982 Birmingham shivered under its coldest night since records began. The all-time low of -20°C (-4°F), was recorded at Birmingham International Airport. It was -27.2°C in Scotland, equalling the lowest temperature ever recorded in the UK.

Arctic conditions in January 2004 caused the worst ever traffic conditions in the city after widespread ice caught gritters by surprise. 'Outrage' was the headline in the local paper.

In January 1968 Birmingham was hit by a blizzard that caused traffic chaos until 11.00 p.m. Councillors said such chaos should never happen again . . . it did.

A whirlwind, which became known as Birmingham Bertha, tore through the city on 4 April 1877.

A huge whirlwind ripped through the Sparkbrook, Small Heath and Bordesley Green districts on 14 June 1931 leaving more than 100 families homeless.

A twister moved through Selly Oak and Stirchley in July 1999 prompting 400 emergency calls to the fire service.

A tornado with speeds of up to 136mph ripped through parts of the city in 2005. It lasted for about four minutes and caused widespread damage particularly in the Sparkbrook, Moseley and Kings Heath areas.

Birmingham had its hottest day ever in July 2007 when temperatures reached 34.9°C, 95°F, beating a record set in August 2003.

JOSEPH CHAMBERLAIN FACTFILE

Joseph Chamberlain was born in London in 1836.

When he was eighteen he moved to Birmingham to work for relatives at Nettlefold's screw manufactory.

He married Harriet Kenrick in 1861. They had two children, Beatrice and Austen.

Beatrice died in the influenza epidemic at the end of the First World War.

Harriet died just a few days after giving birth to her second child, Austen.

Austen grew up to become Chancellor of the Exchequer.

Joseph got remarried in 1868 to Florence Kenrick, a cousin of Harriet's.

They had four children: Neville, Ida, Hilda and Ethel.

Neville was to become mayor 1915–16 before rising to become Prime Minister at the outbreak of the Second World War.

Harriet died while giving birth to their fifth child.

Joseph became interested in civic affairs and joined the council in 1868.

He became mayor in 1873 and a Liberal MP for the city in 1876. However, he split with the party over Gladstone's support for Irish Home Rule.

From 1895 to 1906 he was Conservative Secretary of State for the colonies.

He lived at Highbury Hall in Moseley.

In 1906 there were tremendous celebrations to mark his seventieth birthday.

Shortly after his seventieth birthday he suffered a stroke and his work was reduced.

He died in 1914 and was buried in Key Hill Cemetery.

INTERESTING FIRST CITIZENS

Birmingham's mayor in 1847 was Charles Geach, founder of the Midland Bank. He died at the age of forty-six in 1854 from what was described as 'a combination of physical disorders including chronic diarrhoea and the after effects of a kick from a hansom cab horse.'

Freda Cocks became the first Conservative lord mayor in 1977 and 1978 and the first chairwoman of major city council. She was also the first female to receive the freedom of the city. She was a councillor in Quinton for over thirty-five years. She lost her sight and worked tirelessly for the Royal Institute for the Blind.

Moseley-born Harold Blumenthal, lord mayor in Brum's centenary year of 1989, later became the only commoner to appear on a postage stamp with the queen. The photograph that was used showed the lord mayor and queen in Birmingham and was used two years later by the Commonwealth country of Grenada on the stamps to mark the monarch's sixty-fifth birthday. No one apparently noticed that a commoner was on the design and he went down in history.

Sir William Bowater, born in Kidsgrove, moved to Birmingham when he was six with his father who was a dental surgeon. William got his teeth into politics and became a major figure on the local political scene. He was a councillor for over forty years and was five times lord mayor and led the city through the First World War.

The lady mayoress in 2003, Deirdre Alden, herself a Birmingham councillor, can claim to have been a top draw for thirty years because she drew illustrations for the girls' magazine *Bunty*.

In August 1859 Birmingham elected an MP without him ever coming into the town. His name was John Bright, a leading politician who had lost his seat in Manchester. The town wanted a major well-known figure to stand and looked to Bright, who agreed, and his election address was rushed out without him having time to get to Brum. News of his success was sent to him in Rochdale!

William Whitehouse Collins was born in Harborne, which was then in Staffordshire, in September 1853 and moved to New Zealand in 1890. He became an MP for Christchurch and died in Sydney in April 1923.

Henry Allcock was from Edgbaston and was a judge and member of parliament in Canada. He died of a fever in Quebec in 1808, while in office.

Former lord mayor Denis Martineau, who passed away in 1999, was reputed to have been the world's only fifth-generation civic head. He was preceded by his great grandfather Robert Martineau 1840 and Sir Thomas Martineau in 1884–7, who was knighted by Queen Victoria when she opened the Law Courts. Then came his grandfather Ernest

Martineau in 1912 and his father Wilfred Martineau 1940. Denis was lord mayor from 1986 to 1987.

WARTIME

During one of Birmingham's three Zeppelin raids, bombs were dropped in fields between Fox Hollies Road and Shirley Road. In February 1916, 35 people, including the lady mayoress of Walsall, were killed when nine Zeppelins penetrated inland, missed Birmingham, and dropped bombs across parts of the Black Country. Walsall's war memorial is located at the spot where she died.

The Birmingham Small Arms Company (BSA) supplied Lewis guns to the British Army. Production increased from 30 guns per week in 1914 to 2,000 per week by 1918. US Army Colonel Isaac Newton Lewis designed the automatic machine gun.

A marble tablet in the corridor leading to the reception of the Council House reads, 'A memorial of gratitude to the Citizens of Birmingham dedicated by Belgian exiles as a testimony to the generous spirit of amity which they received in this City during the years of the Great war 1914–1918'.

The Hall of Memory was built to commemorate the 12,320 Birmingham citizens who died and the 35,000 who were wounded in the First World War. When the Prince of Wales laid the foundation stone, on 12 June 1923, he said the building would stand to 'symbolise to generations to come that Birmingham stood for, during a period of great national crisis – work of every kind unflinchingly given, compassion to the sick and wounded, courage and resource in adversity, and, above all, self-sacrifice in the face of death.'

THE EIGHT VICTORIA CROSS WINNERS WHO ARE BURIED IN BIRMINGHAM & SOLIHULL

James Cooper won his Victoria Cross off the Andaman Islands in 1867 and is buried at Warstone Lane Cemetery.

Alfred Knight won his VC at Gravenstafel Ridge near Ypres, Belgium, in 1917 and is buried at New Oscott College.

George Onions won his VC at Achiet-le-Petit, France, in 1918 and is buried at Quinton Cemetery.

George Ravenhill won his VC at Colenso in South Africa in 1889 and is buried at Witton Cemetery.

Arthur Vickers won his VC at Hulloch Quarries, France, in 1915 and is buried at Witton Cemetery.

Thomas Turrall won his VC at La Boiselle, Somme, France, in 1916 and is buried at Robin Hood Cemetery, Solihull.

Sir Arnold Waters won his VC at Ors, France, in 1918 and is buried at Sutton Coldfield Crematorium.

Alfred Wilcox won his VC at Laventie, France, in 1918 and is buried at St Peter & St Paul Church, Aston.

BRUM AT WAR

Chief Spitfire pilot, Alex Henshaw, based at Castle Bromwich, was threatened with arrest by the police after a PR stunt over the city centre. In September 1940 a captured Messerschmitt was put on show next to the Hall of Memory and huge crowds gathered to see it, raising funds in the process for the Lord Mayor's Spitfire Fund. Alex took part in a spectacular flypast and performed a low-level Victory Roll, which pleased the crowd but not the police as he roared off over New Street!

A trawler named *Aston Villa* was one of sixteen built for Consolidated Fisheries Ltd of Grimsby that were named after football teams. It was taken over by the Admiralty on 29 September 1939. She was heavily damaged on 30 April 1940 by a German dive bomber in Kroken Bay near Namsos, Norway, and was scuttled on 3 May 1940.

It was reported in October 1942 that 25,000 Birmingham houses needed to have their windows replaced due to bomb damage. The council said, 'If we are to replace only 50 per cent of the broken windows with a staff of 250 men, it will take 21 weeks to do the job.'

There were 77 air raids on the city and 2,241 citizens of Birmingham died between 8 August 1940 and 23 April 1943.

Members of the Birmingham Air Raids Remembrance Association helped raise funds for a sculpture known as the Tree of Life. It was erected in the Bullring in memory of the 2,241 civilian victims of the raids in the Second World War. Over 3,000 people attended the ceremony in October 2005.

Around 2,000 tons of bombs were dropped on Birmingham, making it the third most heavily bombed city in the United Kingdom.

BIRMINGHAM IN NUMBERS

THE ONE MAN AND HIS DOG

Flash was Birmingham's first police dog, in 1951, and his handler was
PC J. Ford.

THE FIRST TWO MEMBERS OF PARLIAMENT IN 1832

Thomas Attwood
Joshua Scholefield

THE THREE FEMALE OTTERS AT THE NATIONAL SEALIFE CENTRE

Apricot
Kiwi
Mango

THE FOUR PRESENTERS OF ATV's *THE GOLDEN SHOT*

Jackie Rae 1967
Bob Monkhouse 1968–71 and 1975
Norman Vaughan 1972
Charlie Williams 1973–4

THE FIVE ROADS THAT FORMED THE BIRMINGHAM SUPERPRIX CIRCUIT

Pershore Street
Sherlock Street
Belgrave Middleway
Bristol Street
Bromsgrove Street

THE SIX AREAS WHICH BECAME PART OF BIRMINGHAM IN 1911

Aston
Erdington
Handsworth
Kings Norton
Northfield
Yardley

THE SEVEN DISTRICTS OF BIRMINGHAM

City Core
Eastside
Digbeth
Southside & Highgate
Westside & Ladywood
Jewellery Quarter
Gunsmith Quarter

These are designated in the city's new twenty-year development called the Big City Plan.

THE EIGHT ITEMS IN THE MILLENNIUM POINT TIME CAPSULE

Italy: Miniature model of a Ferrari
Japan: An Emros Microrobot, the world's smallest robot
Canada: Four objects: a piece from the Sudbury Neutrino
    Observatory, seeds, a book on innovation and an encyclopaedia
    on a CD-ROM
Germany: Brandenburg Gate tile
France: Miniature model of the euro train 'Le Shuttle'
USA: Digital Library of information about the USA
Russia: Model of the Sputnik satellite
UK: computer chip

THE NINE CHURCH OF ENGLAND BISHOPS OF BIRMINGHAM

Charles Gore	1905–11
Henry Russell Wakefield	1911–24
Ernest William Barnes	1924–53
John Leonard Wilson	1953–69
Lawrence Ambrose Brown	1969–77
Hugh William Montefore	1977–87
Mark Santer	1987–2002
John Tucker Mugabi Sentamu	2002–5
David Urquhart	2006–present

THE TEN ITEMS IN THE INTERNATIONAL CONVENTION CENTRE'S TIME CAPSULE

Souvenir tie from the NEC
ICC Commemorative medal
CBSO baton signed by orchestra conductor Simon Rattle
Commemorative coin given out on the opening night of Symphony Hall
Pair of autographed ballet shoes belonging to the Birmingham Royal
    Ballet's principal dancer, Marion Tait
Handcrafted gold ring from the Jewellery Quarter
A print reproduction by pre-Raphaelite painter Rossetti called
    'Proserpine' from the Museum & Art Gallery
Luggage tag bearing the name Birmingham International Airport
Football signed by players of Aston Villa Football Club
The historic issue of the *Daily News* marking the end of the Gulf War

THE ELEVEN PLAYERS THAT STARTED THE 1982 EUROPEAN CUP FINAL

Aston Villa beat Bayern Munich 1–0.

Jimmy Rimmer (he was replaced by Nigel Spink)
Kenny Swain
Gary Williams
Allan Evans
Kenny McNaught
Dennis Mortimer
Des Bremner
Gary Shaw
Peter Withe
Gordon Cowans
Tony Morley

THE TWELVE ROADS THAT MAKE UP THE INNER RING ROAD

St Chads Queensway
Lancaster Street Queensway
St Chads Circus Queensway
Paradise Circus Queensway
Great Charles Queensway
Suffolk Street Queensway
Holloway Circus Queensway
Smallbrook Queensway
St Martin's Circus Queenway
Moor Street Queensway
James Watt Queensway
Masshouse Circus Queensway

THE THIRTEEN CITY HOTELS LISTED IN BIRMINGHAM'S 1966 WORLD CUP BROCHURE

Albany, Smallbrook Queensway
Arden, New Street
Briars, 176–8 Hagley Road
Cobden, 166–70 Hagley Road
Grand, Colmore Row

Grosvenor House, 51–9 Hagley Road
Imperial, Temple Street
Lambert Court, 336 Hagley Road
Market, Station Street
Midland, New Street
New Victoria Street, 34 Corporation Street
Norfolk, 259–67 Hagley Road
Waverley, New Meeting Street

THE FOURTEEN BIRMINGHAM AREA PEOPLE WORTH £400M OR MORE

According to the *Birmingham Post* Rich List 2010

Kirsty Bertarelli	£5.0bn	Pharmaceuticals
John Caudwell	£1.5bn	Telecommunications
Sir Anthony Bamford	£1.0bn	Manufacturing
Viscount Portman	£950m	Property
Randy Lerner	£900m	Finance/Sport
Jorgen Philip-Sorensen	£620m	Security
Felix Dennis	£580m	Publishing
Lord Paul of Marylebone & Family	£500m	Manufacturing
John Bloor	£500m	Construction/Manufacturing
Tony Gallagher	£500m	Construction
Jacques Gaston Murray	£480m	Manufacturing
Freddie Linnett & Family	£450m	Construction
The Mackie Family	£450m	Electrical

THE FIFTEEN BIRMINGHAM POETS LAUREATE

Brian Lewis (1996/7)
David Hart (1997/8)
Sibyl Ruth (1998/9)
Simon Pitt (1999/2000)
Roshan Doug (2000/01)
Roi Kwabena(2001/02)
Julie Boden (2002/03)
Roz Goddard (2003/04)
Don Barnard (2004/05)
Richard Grant (2005/06)

Giovanni Esposito (2006/7)
Charlie Jordan (2007/8)
Chris Morgan (2008/9)
Adrian Johnson (2009/10)
Roy Mc Farlane (2010/11)

THE SIXTEEN THINGS ON
THE CHARM BRACELET TRAIL

A walking trail along Newhall Street and Frederick Street to the Jewellery Quarter. Plaques depicting points of interest are located on the floor next to key buildings.

The Key: This starts and unlocks the trail.

Silent Boots: These were made for policemen in the area in the 1890s so they could pounce on thieves.

Rip Van Winkle: This story was written by Washington Irving when he was in the area in 1818.

Chartists Meeting Point: In 1832, 200,000 people gathered to campaign for parliamentary reform.

The FA Cup: The first FA Cup was designed in the area.

Whistles: J. Hudson Ltd make whistles, most famously used by the crew on the *Titanic* and by football referees.

Matthew Boulton: A commemoration of the famous industrialist.

Turkish Bath: The factory used recycled steam from the nearby baths.

Anchor: This commemorates the assay office established in 1773 which had the anchor logo.

Nibs: 75 per cent of the world's nibs were produced in the pen factory.

The Hockley Flyer: This honours the trade magazine produced in the area.

Shrapnel: This is located outside one of the factories bombed in the Second World War.

Spitfire: Spitfire parts were among items built for the war effort.

School of Jewellery: The school opened in 1890.

Peas like Emeralds: Once the location of a restaurant, the menu of which included 'small new peas like emeralds'.

Chamberlain Clock: This clock was erected in 1903 to commemorate the work of Joseph Chamberlain.

THE SEVENTEEN PLACES ON THE MATTHEW BOULTON WALK

Colmore Square at Steelhouse Lane: Plaque to denote his birthplace.

Old Square: Birmingham's finest Georgian square in Boulton's day.

St Philip's Cathedral: Boulton was christened there in 1728 and his mother buried there in 1787.

Birmingham Museum & Art Gallery: This features a collection of Boulton's wares.

Central Library: Several million of his business letters and documents are in the archives.

Broad Street at Centenary Square: Boulton is on the golden statue with Murdock and Watt.

Brindleyplace and canals: Boulton was an early investor in the canal network and his wares were shipped all over the world.

Farmer's Bridge and Birmingham & Fazeley Canal: Canal nearest to the Jewellery Quarter and Boulton's home on Newhall Hill. It was demolished in 1787.

Birmingham Assay Office: Boulton helped in the campaign to get this established.

St Paul's Square: Boulton worshipped in the Church of St Paul's.

Museum of the Jewellery Quarter: Metalworking techniques from Boulton's days are demonstrated there.

Think Tank, Millennium Point: Boulton & Watt's Smethwick Engine, the oldest working steam engine in the world, is on show.

Soho Foundry, Smethwick: Built for the construction of Boulton & Watt steam engines in 1796.

Soho House, Handsworth: Home of Matthew Boulton from 1766 until his death in 1809, after which he was moved elsewhere!

St Mary's Parish Church, Handsworth: Boulton, Watt and Murdoch are all buried there.

Aston Hall: It was leased at one time to the Watt family, Boulton's business partner.

Sarehole Mill: Boulton leased it between 1756 and 1761.

THE EIGHTEEN STREETS IN BRUM IN 1553

Bordesley
Chappell Street
Dale End
Dale End Barrs
Deretend
Dudwall Lane
Dygbeth
Edgbaston Street
English Market
High Street
Little Park Street
Mercer Street
Molle Street
New Street
Priors Conyngre Street
Swan Alley
Welch Market
Well Street

THE FIRST NINETEEN INDIVIDUALS ON THE BROAD STREET WALK OF STARS

Ozzy Osbourne
Noddy Holder
Norman Painting
Tony Brown
Gil Merrick
Julie Walters
Lenny Henry
Joan Armatrading
David Bintley
Bev Bevan
Jasper Carrott
Murray Walker
Tony Iommi
Frank Skinner
Ray Graydon
Gary Newbon
Beverley Knight
Chris Tarrant
Roy Wood

THE TWENTY
SWIMMING BATHS IN THE CITY IN 1986

Aston
Balsall Heath
Bournville
Castle Vale
Erdington
Great Barr
Handsworth
Harborne
Kings Heath
Kingstanding

Monument Road
Nechells
Northfield
Saltley
Selly Oak
Small Heath
Sparkhill
Stechford
Stirchley
Sutton Coldfield

BIRMINGHAM: 1–30

1

Dorothea Waddingham was the only female to be hanged at Winson Green prison. She made the noose headlines on 16 April 1936 after she was convicted of the murder of two patients at a nursing home she ran near Nottingham.

2

King Charles I spent two nights at Aston Hall immediately before the Battle of Edgehill, the first battle in the Civil War. He was travelling from Shrewsbury to London and spent the nights of 16 and 17 October at Aston.

3

Villa Park had the honor of staging three games during the 1966 World Cup finals.

4

William Mills patented and manufactured the Mills bomb (a hand grenade) at the Mills Munition Factory in Birmingham. At first the grenade was fitted with a 7-second fuse, this delay proved too long, giving defenders time to escape the explosion, or even to throw the grenade back, and the time was reduced to 4 seconds.

5

Birmingham group Traffic's debut single, 'Paper Sun', reached number 5 in the charts in April 1967 and Jasper Carrott reached number 5 with 'Funky Moped' in August 1975. Also The Beatles appeared five times on tour in Birmingham.

6
In 1984 Didier Six became the first continental player to play in the Aston Villa first team.

7
The Aston Expressway opened in May 1972 with seven lanes, including a tidal flow system on the centre lane which serves to reduce congestion.

8
The Broad Street pub the Figure of Eight is named after the nearby canal network, the Midlands canal network forming a figure of eight shape centred on the nearby Gas Street Basin.

9

In December 2009 Bernard Longley became the ninth Roman Catholic Archbishop of Birmingham.

10

There are currently ten types of chocolate in each box of Cadbury's Roses.

11

Mitchells & Butlers' most famous beer was Brew XI advertised with the slogan 'for the men of the Midlands'.

12

Birmingham built its first twelve-storey block of flats at Great Francis Street, Nechells, in 1954.

13

Joe Bradford of Birmingham City holds their record for the number of hat-tricks scored – thirteen in total.

14

The dining room at Matthew Boulton's Soho House was equipped with fourteen mahogany chairs in 1798.

15

The Birmingham Botanical Gardens extend to 15 acres and is situated in Edgbaston.

16

Sampson Lloyd established Lloyd's Bank – perhaps he needed the money as he had sixteen children to look after.

17

Only seventeen of the fifty rioters who had been charged were ever brought to trial following the Priestley Riots of 1791; four were convicted, of whom one was pardoned, two were hanged, and the fourth was transported to Botany Bay.

18

There are three eighteen-hole golf courses at The Belfry – the Brabazon course, the PGA National Course and the Derby Course.

19

The Midland Red bus company, formed in 1905, had an initial motorbus fleet of nineteen double-decker buses.

20

Sir Laurence Olivier started his theatre career at the Birmingham Repertory Theatre and while there he performed in twenty productions.

21

Twenty-one shillings, or one guinea, was the price of John Baskerville's first book printed using Baskerville type. It was an edition of poems by Virgil and was said to be 'one of the finest specimens of typography'.

22

When Blackburn Rovers beat West Bromwich Albion in January 2011, twenty-two different nationalities of player participated in the match, a Premier League record.

23

Matthew Boulton owned pew number 23 in St Paul's Church in the Jewellery Quarter.

24

The Jewellery Quarter deals in 24 carat gold, or pure gold. The Farmers' Market at the Jewellery Quarter, which meets on the third Saturday of the month, is called the 24 Carrots Farmers' Market. Geddit?

25

There were twenty-five competing countries in the Eurovision Song Contest when it was held in Birmingham in 1998.

26

The longest bus route in Birmingham is the no. 11 Outer Circle which has a 26-mile route.

27

There were twenty-seven burials in Birmingham in 1555 (and fifteen weddings).

28

In 1847 the death rate in Birmingham was 28 per 1,000; by 1910 it had dropped to 13 and today stands at 7.9 per cent. Not bad, unless you happen to be in the 7.9 per cent.

29

In 2011 the Association of Public Health Observatories named Birmingham as the European Union's 'fattest city'. 29 per cent of the adult population are classified as obese, more than twice that of the European average of 14 per cent.

30

There are thirty operating theatres in the recently opened Queen Elizabeth Hospital.

RANDOM NUMBERS

In 1950 the City Police force had a vehicle fleet of 71 cars, 31 vans and one lorry; 46 of the vehicles were fitted with radios.

In 1925 an orchid at the Botanical Gardens made horticultural history by producing a spike with 43 flowers.

In January 2011 522,562 people flew in and out of Birmingham Airport.

On 16 April 1995 Birmingham's telephone dialling code changed from 021 to 0121.

Bartley Green Reservoir is around 60ft deep at the dam. It was formally opened by the lord mayor in July 1930. It contains 501 million gallons of water.

In July 1973 Edgbaston was the host for the first ever Women's Cricket World Cup, England beating Australia by 92 runs in the final. Enid Bakewell top scored with 118. This contest was inaugurated 2 years before the men's competition.

The no. 11 bus route which carries 50,000 passengers each day is the longest bus route in Europe. There are 266 bus stops on the route that serves 233 places of education, 69 leisure and community facilities, 40 pubs, 19 retail centres, 6 hospitals and 1 prison.

In 1946 it was recorded that only 537 out of 13,000 homes were without a bathroom in Northfield.

In 1968, out of the male entrants to Birmingham City Police, 3 were university graduates, 10 had one or more A levels, 87 had one or more O levels, 29 had one or more other type of certificate and 44 had no educational qualifications.

By the mid-eighteenth century, Erdington had a population of under 700 and within its boundaries were 52 roads, one forge, 40 farms, 96 cottages, 2 smithies and a shop.

The Birmingham Botanical Gardens opened in 1832 and within two years they had over 9,000 species – 42 donors sent in over 2,400 plants and 10 donors sent in over 1,300 seeds.

64,800 bars of Cadbury's Dairy Milk chocolate bars can be wrapped in one hour.

The Pallasades Shopping Centre, opened in 1971, averages 420,000 visitors per week and has over 90 retail units.

The National Exhibition Centre has 21 halls totalling 200,000 square metres of exhibition space on a 650-acre site. Over 4 million people visit it each year; most of them are still trying to get out of the car park!

Births to mothers born overseas increased from 4,405 in 2001 to 6,699 in 2009, a rise of 55.1 per cent. This compares with an increase of 6.1 per cent for UK-born mothers.

Women aged 40 and over have seen the highest percentage increase in the number of births 2001–9. 318 babies were born to mothers aged 40 or over in 2001 and this figure rose to 533 in 2009.

A medical inspection of Birmingham's school children in 1914 revealed that of the 33,193 examined, 3,943 had vision problems, 1,197 had defective hearing, 3,039 had tonsil or adenoid defects and 92 had a hernia problem. It is not known how many had all four defects!

At the twentieth anniversary of the National Exhibition Centre in 1996 it was revealed that in an average year visitors eat their way through 76,000 doughnuts, 166,000lb of chicken and turkey and 97,000lb of sausages, all washed down with 2½ million cups of coffee, 7½ million cups of tea and 106,000 gallons of draught beer. Then they visited the exhibitions!

Over 7 million people live within one hour's drive of Birmingham; hopefully most will head to the city's bookshops to buy this book!

5

FIRSTS & LASTS

VICTORIAN FIRSTS

The first successful transatlantic telegraph cable was made by James Horsfall at his factory in Hay Mills in 1858. The cable was wrapped in wire that if laid end to end would stretch for an estimated 30,000 miles, and weighed 1,600 tons. It took 250 workers eleven months to manufacture and it was laid on the seabed by Brunel's steamship the *Great Eastern* in fourteen days. Horsfall was also a major exporter of piano wire.

The Great Western Arcade off Colmore Row, opened in 1876, was Birmingham's first arcade. It was built on a site created by the construction of the Great Western Railway tunnel, which runs into the nearby station at Snow Hill.

John Hall Edwards devised the first x-rays in 1896 when he x-rayed the hand of a seamstress, Mrs Berry, showing a needle that had become stuck in her hand. In 1908 he had to have his left arm amputated owing to over exposure to x-rays, as he had used his hand so many times to demonstrate his work! He donated his amputated arm to Birmingham University's Medical School.

On 6 January 1873, surgeon Sampson Gamgee first raised the suggestion that everyone should work overtime to raise money for hospitals on a particular annual Saturday afternoon, to be called Hospital Saturday. This new scheme called the Birmingham Hospital Saturday Fund was inaugurated on 15 March 1873.

The first public trial in Birmingham of a 'horseless carriage' or motor car took place at Cannon Hill Park in 1896. The vehicle was said to have had 'strong cycle wheels, best solid tyres and steel springs'.

Joseph Lucas of Birmingham made what was probably the first rechargeable accumulator-powered cycle lamp in February 1888.

Paper confetti was introduced to the country in August 1896 and first used at the Moseley Botanical Gardens. Most of it was probably thrown away!

Burbury Park in Nechells, which opened in 1877, was the first children's park in the city and one of the first in the country.

The owner of the first telephone in town was Henry Piercy of the Broad Street Engine Works, who had a phone installed in the summer of 1879.

The first telephone exchange opened in November 1879 even though there were less than a dozen subscribers.

The first telephone directory was printed in 1886 at a time when there were 602 subscribers.

By 1882 the telephone company had attracted its first 100 customers and had moved into a new home in the attic of a music shop at the corner of Bennetts Hill and Colmore Row.

Birmingham became the first town in the world to install an underground cable in 1883, which led from Bennett's Hill up to Great Charles Street.

INTERESTING, VERY INTERESTING

The Carlton Cinema, Balsall Heath, was the first in Birmingham to have a lift to the circle.

In 1967 Ladywood's roller rink became the first British venue to host the World Roller Skating Championships.

The City's first three-storey municipal flats were built, in Dutch style, in 1927 at Garrison Lane near St Andrews football ground.

Central Avenue in Longbridge is rumoured to be the first dual carriageway in Birmingham, but city records state the honour goes to Pebble Mill Road, which became a dual carriageway in 1920.

The city's first smoke-free zone was established in 1954 and the last ones came into force in September 1986.

The first parish fire engine came into use in 1695 under the charge of the appropriately named William Burn!

In 1932, Leonard Parsons was the first to use synthetic vitamin C as a treatment for scurvy in children.

St Chad's Circus was the home of the Golden Cross Inn where the owner, Richard Ketley, founded the first known building society in the world in 1775.

Birmingham's first modern factory building was Matthew Boulton's Soho manufactory, established in 1761.

The first MP to be killed in the Second World War was Ronald Cartland, MP for Kings Norton and brother of novelist Barbara Cartland.

The Birmingham Super Prix of 1986 was the first car race around the streets of a British city.

In the mid-1930s there was a club called the First Nighter Club. It aimed to encourage theatregoers to attend first nights and encourage theatre-going habits.

The first member of the royal family to visit the International Convention Centre was Prince Edward. He attended a youth music festival in April 1991 two months before his mum popped by to officially open the centre.

Birmingham's first purpose-built gaol was in Peck Lane, just off New Street in the town centre. The town's first historian, William Hutton, described the lane as, 'crowded with dwellings, filth and distress without.'

Birmingham's first canal, linking the town with the coalmines of the Black Country, was opened on 6 November 1769. There was great rejoicing in Birmingham and even church bells rang out. The price of coal immediately fell creating an economic boom adding to the prosperity of the town.

The first man to install gas lights outside his factory was Josiah Pemberton, who was a businessman who made gas lighting equipment – all very enlightening for a man who enjoyed light work.

Birmingham's Blood Transfusion Service opened in 1925 and a Rover Scout, Henry Leader, was the first to give blood. In 1934 the lord mayor gave a medallion to the first eight people to give blood ten times.

In 1953 Grosvenor House at 56 New Street became the first postwar city centre building to be completed.

In November 1965 Brummie-born broadcaster, theatre critic and writer Kenneth Tynan achieved, if that's the right word, the dubious honour of being the first person to use the four-letter 'F' word on television. It was a deliberate attempt to push the boundaries of speech on TV. The public outcry was immense and it was even discussed in Parliament.

The first manufacturer of the Robertson's Jam Golly badge was R.E.V. Gomm, who are still making badges in Birmingham today.

Lisa Clayton was the first woman to sail single-handed and non-stop around the world. She set sail in September 1994 in the vessel *Spirit of Birmingham* on a 285-day trip.

Birmingham was the first UK city to have a motorway route into its centre. This is known as the Aston Expressway or A38M.

Shard End Library, opened in 1967, was the first in Birmingham to use plastic membership cards instead of the traditional card tickets.

The first Norman knight who lived in Weoley Castle was said to be called Paganel. The nearby junior school in Swinford Road is named Paganel Junior School in his honour.

Brylcreem was first manufactured at the County Chemical Company on Bradford Street in 1928. It was first advertised on TV by the jingle, 'Brylcreem, A Little Dab'll Do Ya!' It has been claimed that the famous 'Yabba Dabba Doo' of *Flintstones* fame was inspired by Brylcreem's jingle. Al Reed, who was the voice artist for Fred Flintstone on the programme, was supposed to have shouted 'Yahoo!' but thought 'Yabba Dabba Doo' sounded better.

A £200 Gucci handbag made the news in 2003 when it became the first item purchased in the newly opened Selfridge's building in the Bullring. 6,000 people visted the shop in the first hour of it being open.

Birmingham's first mosque was opened in 1943 in a house at the lower end of Edward Road, Balsall Heath, to serve the needs of a small Yemeni population.

The final round of the first ever televised leaders' debates, hosted by the BBC, was held at Birmingham University during the 2010 General Election campaign.

TOP BIRMINGHAM LASTS

The last village pound in Birmingham stands in Northfield next to the Great Stone Inn. It had been a repository for stray animals since the sixteenth century, although it is no longer used. A large glacial boulder dug up from nearby now stands in the pound. The pub claims to be able to sell 'by the pint, by the pound and by the stone'.

The last 'spot the ball' competition in the *Birmingham Evening Mail* and *Sunday Mercury*, game 1296A, was held on 26 May 1996, although it was briefly revived during the 2010 World Cup.

Birmingham-born Captain Henry Lockhart St John Fancourt was a naval aviator, and held important aviation commands with the Fleet Air Arm during the Second World War. When he died at the age of 103, in 2004, he was the last survivor who had actively been involved in the Battle of Jutland.

Andrew Bromwich, a priest who lived at Oscott House on the site of the present Maryvale, was arrested in 1679 and became the last Catholic priest in England to be sentenced to death. The sentence was suspended and he spent nine years in prison.

The last tram ran on 4 July 1953. It trundled from Steelhouse Lane to Erdington and Short Heath. The lord mayor, Alderman Crump, took the controls for part of the journey; fittingly he was a former tram driver. The last remaining piece of tram track in the city centre has been preserved in Edmund Street.

Birmingham's last gas lamp streetlight was switched off on New Year's Eve 1974. In the 1930s over 100 men maintained the 35,000 lights, each with a round of 250 lamp standards. The first such lights dated back to 1816. The last one was removed from Duke Street, Gosta Green. No doubt some took a dim view of this, but the bright sparks in the electricity department soon brightened everyone's lives.

The last surviving back-to-back houses in the city at Court 15 Inge Street are three pairs of back-to-back houses and five back houses. They are now owned by the National Trust which runs them as a tourist attraction.

On 21 June 1965, a horse called Plantation Inn finished last in the last ever race at Bromford Bridge, Birmingham's racecourse, which was Brum's last ever racecourse.

The last town crier, 'Old Jacob' Jacob Wilson, rang his last bell (Oyez he did) on 18 January 1882. He had been a crier for fifty-two years and his father was the official crier for fifty years before that. That's a century of being big noises in the town, and that was worth shouting about!

The Beatles last appeared on tour in Birmingham on 9 December 1965 at the Odeon, New Street. The same year they visited Brum to appear on *Thank Your Lucky Stars*.

In October 2003 thousands of spectators filled Birmingham International Airport to watch the last appearance of Concorde as part of its farewell tour before being taken out of service.

The last of 12,000 Spitfires flew off the production line at the Castle Bromwich Factory in 1946. It was numbered PK 726.

LEISURE

TEN TOP BIRMINGHAM PARKS

Queen Victoria opened Aston Hall and Park in 1858. The press noted all classes of people watched 'with absorbing interest'.

Calthorpe Park was named after Lord Calthorpe and was the town's first park in 1857. There was a reception in the Town Hall and procession to the park with a 21-gun salute at the opening.

Cannon Hill Park was, more or less, the back garden of benefactor Louisa Ryland – presumably she didn't like cutting the grass as it was handed over to the city and opened as a park in 1873. At her request there was no official opening ceremony.

Handsworth Park opened in 1889 but was outside the city boundary until 1911. It became famous for shows and exhibitions.

Highgate Park was the first open space bought directly by the council for recreational activities. During the Second World War over 200 bombs fell on it causing £10,000 of damage.

Kings Heath Park is well known for its horticultural training school and TV garden set up by ATV in 1972. *Gardening Today* became a popular programme under the cultivated tones of Bob Price and Cyril Fletcher.

Queen's Park, Harborne, was opened with help of money raised during Queen Victoria's Golden Jubilee celebrations of 1887. A Garden for the Blind opened there during the present Queen's coronation celebrations in 1953.

Small Heath Park opened in 1878 and has rarely closed since, except for the day when Queen Victoria passed by in 1887 and 5,000 children lined the carriage drive to welcome her on her way to open the Law Courts.

Summerfield Park opened in 1876 in the former grounds of Lucas Chance, wealthy glass manufacturer. The park held Birmingham's first bonfire carnival in 1960.

Ward End Park was opened in the former grounds of Ward End House, home to the town's first historian William Hutton. The unemployed residents of the area built a boating pool in 1908–9.

A DOZEN GREAT NAMES FOR PHILANTHROPIC INSTITUTIONS IN 1937

Association for the Care and Training of Unmarried Mothers and their Babies
Association of the Ladies of Charity of the Archdiocese of Birmingham
Birmingham Diocesan Clergy Aid Fund and Clergy Widows' and Orphans' Fund
Birmingham and District Licensed Victuallers' Asylum
Church of England Waifs and Strays Society
Church Schools Masters' and School Mistresses' Benevolent Institution
Diocesan Council for Moral Welfare (Rescue & Preventative)
Ladies' Association for the Care of Friendless Girls
Midland Counties Institution Training Home for Feeble-Minded Boys
Police Added Association for Clothing Poor Children
The Agatha Stacey Homes for Mentally Deficient Young Women
The Samuel Welsh Memorial Homes for Aged and Incapacitated Nurses

HALF A DOZEN GREAT-NAMED SOCIETIES IN 1937

Birmingham Gardeners' Mutual Improvement Society
The English Folk Dance and Song Society
National Association of Cemetery and Crematorium Superintendents
Shakespeare Memorial Library Committee of Subscribers
Society for the Propagation of the Gospel in Foreign Parts
Society of Yorkshire Folk in Birmingham

SOME BIRMINGHAM CLUBS THAT YOU MAY, OR MAY NOT, HAVE BEEN AWARE OF

Birmingham University Board Games Society

Sutton Scrabble Club

The British Chelonia Group, Midlands Group (dedicated to the conservation and care of tortoises, terrapins and turtles!)

Midland Counties Poodle Club

Midland Zebra Finch Club

North Birmingham Cage Bird Society

Beekeepers' Association of Birmingham

The Birmingham and District Carnation Society

Birmingham Saturday Federation Pigeon Club

Birmingham Fur Fanciers Society

The Midland Bonsai Society

Gardeners' Mutual Improvement Society

Tree Lovers League, Birmingham Branch (!)

Forget Me Not Ex-Servicemen's Club

Birmingham Baptist Men's Luncheon Club

Arnold Club (for headmasters)

A40 Farina Club, West Midlands Area

West Midland Movement and Dance Association

Birmingham Enterprise, Cave and Mine Exploration Club

Auricula and Primula Society

Birmingham & District Table Tennis Association

Water Polo Referees' Association

British Petanque Association, West Midlands Region

The Midlands Woodpigeon Club (to provide a crop protection service for farmers against woodpigeon and shooting for members)

LEISURE MISCELLANEOUS

In 1943 Anthony Pratt devised the board game Cluedo, while living in Brandwood Road, Kings Heath, in a house which may have had lead piping and candlesticks.

Birmingham held a visitor survey in 1997 and over 1,100 people were interviewed. The results of the survey showed that:

19 per cent were day visitors from overseas staying in Birmingham overnight.

21 per cent were making their first visit to the city.

84 per cent said the city had improved since their last visit.

The most noted comments were for better and greater number of public toilets and for more pedestrianisation. Since then there has been greater pedestrianisation giving people more flat surfaces along which to look for ever-decreasing numbers of public loos. The city has never been flushed with loos and seems never likely to be.

Birmingham held an annual Tulip Festival in Cannon Hill Park. A windmill from the festival existed until it was burned down in 1995.

Birmingham's first new park for twenty-five years opened near the ICC in May 1993. City Centre Gardens was built on the site of the former lighting depot, though today different bulbs are in evidence on the 2-acre site together with 21 trees and over 7,000 shrubs and plants.

THOSE GOOD OLD RADIO DAYS

On 5 December 1922 station 5IT in Witton began broadcasting *Children's Hour* and almost every other station in the country followed it.

Charles Parker (1921–80) was a pioneering radio producer, based in Birmingham from 1953. The Charles Parker Archive in the Central Library contains over 5,000 recordings.

BBC Radio Birmingham went on air on 9 November 1970 on 95.6 VHF, later adding 206MW, and broadcast across not just Birmingham but Wolverhampton, the Black Country and Coventry as well, so the name was never really appropriate and it eventually became BBC Radio West Midlands, now shortened to BBC WM.

The first voice heard on the station was that of Robert Clifford Joiner, a crying baby born in the early hours of the day the station went on air. Robert is now an actor and has completed an MA in Playwriting at Birmingham University.

Eighteen-year-old Hagley DJ Peter Powell, who presented the Breakfast Show for nine months until he handed over to Les Ross, presented the first programme.

Long-serving presenter Les Ross, real name Leslie Meakin, was a clerk working for Birmingham cemeteries, who sort of went from grave to rave, winning a *Birmingham Evening Mail* DJ competition and beating Johnnie Walker. He was awarded an MBE for services to broadcasting in 1996.

Martin Henfield was the news editor at BBC Radio Birmingham in 1972 and his brother Mike was based at the station's office in Wolverhampton, which was in the Grand Theatre.

Denis McShane, a sports reporter at BBC Radio Birmingham, became an MP in Rotherham and Minister for Europe.

Two well-known television personalities of today both worked together at BBC Radio Birmingham and shared a bleak emergency shift in November 1974. Jim Rosenthal, now of ITV Sport, manned the radio car during the night of the IRA pub bombings, handing over in the early hours of the morning to Nick Owen who went onto anchor TVAM and is now with BBC Midlands Today.

After the name change the first voice heard on BBC Radio West Midlands was that of Alan Dedicoat now famous as the 'voice of the balls' on the lottery programmes on BBC1.

Reproducteur

Enregistreur

The longest-serving presenter is John Platt who joined BBC Radio Birmingham in 1978 and still presents the popular Network Gold programme.

A child member of the team that worked on BBC Radio Birmingham's children's programme Radio Brum Club, Dave Lowe, used his experience to good effect by writing jingles and theme music. He devised the *Midlands Today* theme in 1993 and the current theme tune to *BBC News* was also one of his creations.

On 4 July 2004 BBC Radio WM moved from its Pebble Mill home to the new state-of-the-art broadcasting centre in The Mailbox.

Popular Sunday heritage presenter Carl Chinn was awarded an MBE in 2007 for services to local history and charity work. He has written numerous local history books and newspaper columns.

Birmingham's commercial radio station BRMB went on air on 19 February 1974 on 261MW and 94.8 VHF.

The company behind BRMB was known as Birmingham Broadcasting Ltd, and the name BRMB came from letters from the words BiRMingham Broadcasting.

The very first voice heard on the station was newsman Brian Sheppard, while the former ATV television announcer Kevin Morrison presented the first programme.

Tony Butler was the first sports editor and he pioneered the concept of sports phone-ins, developing a cult following.

Veteran broadcaster Ed Doolan presented two programmes on the opening day and is still broadcasting in the city, now on BBC WM.

BRMB had a sister, Xtra AM, introduced in 1988, but it later became part of Gold – somehow the concept of a local radio station means introducing programmes from London!

BRMB began broadcasting from the former Alpha Television Studios, the home of ATV in Aston, but later moved to Broad Street.

The BRMB theme tune 'Sound Way to Spend Your Day' was written by local musicians Brenda Scott and John Patrick.

GREAT TELLY FROM BIRMINGHAM

The first large-scale, purpose-built TV and radio broadcasting centre was opened by Princess Anne at Pebble Mill in November 1971. She was driven to the studios in an undertaker's limousine, a black Rolls-Royce, ordered by the city council after criticism of an old Austin Princess, a car that had been used by Princess Margaret in the city a few weeks earlier.

TEN PROGRAMMES FROM PEBBLE MILL

A Year in Provence
All Creatures Great and Small
Angels
Boys from the Blackstuff
Good Morning with Anne & Nick
Howard's Way
Juliet Bravo
Nanny
Poldark
Pebble Mill at One

A DOZEN PRESENTERS OF *PEBBLE MILL AT ONE* & *PEBBLE MILL*

Josephine Buchan
Fern Britton
Paul Coia
Tom Coyne
Marion Foster
Bob Langley
Jan Leeming
Donny Macleod
Magnus Magnusson
David Seymour
Judi Spiers
Alan Titchmarsh

The last episode of *Pebble Mill at One* was broadcast on 23 May 1986.

In December 2000 the BBC announced it was to close Pebble Mill and move to a state-of-the-art broadcasting centre at The Mailbox.

BBC MIDLANDS TODAY

The regional news programme began in 1949 but it was revamped on 28 September 1964 when a new 21-minute programme began from a studio in Broad Street. It was presented by Barry Lankester and called *Midlands Today.*

Presenter Nick Owen was one of the first faces to appear on breakfast television in Britain. He is chairman of Luton Town Football Club and presented many major sporting events for ITV Sport. He was the last person to present a live programme from the BBC studios at Pebble Mill when he read the late news on the night the studios closed before moving to The Mailbox in 2004.

Kay Alexander was presented with a special award by the Royal Television Society in 2003 to mark thirty years in television.

Tom Coyne presented the first edition of *Midlands Today* from Pebble Mill in 1971. Earlier he had been the first news reader on Tyne Tees TV, Tom having presented the first bulletin for the station in 1959.

Sue Beardsmore presented the first *Midlands Today* breakfast bulletin in 1983.

At the end of his last news broadcast on *Midlands Today* in July 1997 Alan Towers stunned viewers by saying, 'I would just like to let you know that I am retiring today after 25 years and this is my last broadcast. When I joined the BBC it was led by giants. Now, unfortunately, it is led by pygmies in grey suits wearing blindfolds. How sad.'

Other presenter/ reporters during the programme's history include:

Colin Pemberton
Geoffrey Green
David Davies
Michael Buerk
David Stevens

JUST AN ORDINARY COPPER

The famed PC George Dixon of the 1960s TV series *Dixon of Dock Green* has, I am *policed* to say, a great link with Birmingham.

In the 1870s George Dixon was a real life councillor and Member of Parliament for Birmingham. His great passion was education and he featured prominently on the Birmingham School Board.

A school, which still exists, was named after him.

A former pupil of the school, Michael Balcon became a famous playwright/film director, gaining a knighthood in 1948.

His film *The Blue Lamp* featured a fictional policeman from Dock Green; his name was PC George Dixon, named after Balcon's old school.

The film was a great success and the spin-off TV series *Dixon of Dock Green* ran from 1955 until 1976, not bad for an ordinary copper who was patrolling his beat.

ATV TODAY/CENTRAL NEWS

Central Tonight presenter Bob Warman is the most well-known face on local TV in Birmingham. He began appearing on news programmes in the Midlands in 1973 as a reporter on *ATV Today* which became *Central News*. He presented Britain's first breakfast programme *Good Morning Calendar* in Yorkshire in 1977. He is President of the Birmingham Press Club, which is the world's oldest press club. Bob went to school with Nick Owen who presents *Midlands Today*, the BBC equivalent of *Central News*.

TWENTY WELL-KNOWN FORMER *ATV TODAY* PRESENTERS/REPORTERS

Gwyn Richards	Anne Diamond
Derek Hobson	Llewela Bailey
Michelle Newman	Wendy Nelson
Terry Lloyd	John Swallow
Tony Maycock	Reg Harcourt
Geoff Meade	Terry Thomas
Bob Hall	Gary Newbon
Chris Tarrant	Billy Wright
Jimmy Greaves	Sue Jay
Terry Biddlecombe	Trevor East

CROSSROADS MOTEL, CAN I HELP YOU?

*Crossroad*s was a soap opera about life in a fictional hotel in the village of Kings Oak and 4,510 episodes were filmed in Birmingham between 1964 and 1988. It was revamped and returned from 2001 to 2003.

Star of the show was actress Noele Gordon, so named because she was born on Christmas Day. She played Meg Richardson, later Meg Mortimer. Jane Rossington and Roger Tonge played her screen offspring, Jill and Sandy.

'Crossroads Motel, can I help you?', were the first words spoken on set.

Susan Hanson, the real-life wife of musician Carl Wayne, played a popular waitress, Diane, who married postman Vince Parker in the show.

Another long-running and popular character was Amy Turtle, the cleaner, played by Ann George. She apparently got the part after writing in to complain there were not enough characters with Brummie accents.

Character Wilf Harvey lived in a cottage in Gas Street canal basin next to the ATV studios.

Jane Rossington was the only cast member to be in the first and last episode.

The programme was going to be called *Midland Road*, but the name was changed at the last minute to *Crossroads*, as the programme was to revolve around two sisters, Meg and Kitty, who lived on opposite sides of a crossroads on the fictitious Midland Road.

The first episode included the appearance of a jockey without a horse. The jockey in question was a certain Mrs Jockey, Noele Gordon's mother, who had a walk-on part.

In 1975 motel owner Meg Richardson married Hugh Mortimer and hundreds of fans turned out for the wedding scene filmed in St Philip's Cathedral. It is said that during filming a choirboy was sick in the pews and production had to be suspended. He may well have got sick of the time it was taking; it took about three hours to record!

Tony Hatch devised the famous theme music. The theme featured on Paul McCartney and Wings' album *Venus and Mars*.

The character of the original postmistress Miss Tatum, played by Elisabeth Croft, was based on producer Reg Watson's aunt.

In 1968 Sue Nicholls, who played waitress Marylin Gates, released the single 'Where Will You Be?' which reached number 17 in the pop charts.

DON'T GET IN A TISWAS

Tiswas was a Saturday morning ITV kids' programme which ran from 1974 to 1982.

Tiswas stood for Today Is Saturday Watch And Smile.

It did wonders for the careers of Chris Tarrant, Sally James and Lenny Henry.

The unknown star of the show was the Phantom Flan Flinger.

Children and adults were doused with water, custard and sludge while trapped in cages.

Jasper Carrott appeared and once introduced the 'Dying Fly' dance.

One of the men behind the show, ATV announcer Peter Tomlinson, later became the real life High Sheriff of Nottingham.

ALSO ON THE TELLY

The first series of *The One Show* came from a temporary studio on the canalside at the BBC Mailbox complex in August 2006. The presenters were Birmingham's very own Adrian Chiles and Nadia Sawalha. Later it moved to London without the BBC explaining why its new state-of-the-art broadcasting centre in Birmingham wasn't big enough to house *The One Show*. Birmingham's loss was London's gain and the programme is now one of the most watched on British television.

The hit Sunday teatime programme *The Golden Shot*, which featured people answering questions and firing a crossbow to release a pot of money, reached an audience of up to 17 million, and came from ATV in Birmingham. It ran from 1967 until it shot its final bolt in 1975. The most well-known presenter was Bob Monkhouse who was assisted by Anne Aston and Wei Wei Wong. The man who loaded the crossbow was John Baker who became known as 'Bernie the Bolt'; though originally he was going to be known as 'Baker the Bullet'.

Fred Dineage, who started his media days as a tea boy at the *Birmingham Mail*, was born in the city and was well known for presenting *How!* He is a legendary figure in television in the south as the presenter of the regional news programme on the south coast. He was awarded the OBE in 2010 and his daughter Caroline is MP for Gosport in Hampshire.

Jeremy Paxman of *Newsnight* fame is not a Brummie and probably wouldn't like to be called one, but he did attend a school within the city boundary at Hills Court Prep School near Rednal while his father worked in the city. The *Newsnight* man was six years old at the time. I must interrupt your reading here for more snippets . . .

Howard Brown, a branch manager for the Halifax building society, won a staff competition to appear in a number of their television and print advertisements. He was born and raised in Sheldon and managed their Sheldon branch. Madame Tussauds in London even had a wax statue of him on display.

Detective series *Dalziel & Pascoe*, starring Warren Clarke and Colin Buchanan, began in Birmingham in 1996. Celebrity guest appearances have been made by Jack Dee, Norman Wisdom, Alison Steadman, Tim Healy, David Soul, Ricky Tomlinson, James Bolam, Sanjeev Bhaskar, Prunella Scales and Celia Imrie.

Alan Weeks presented the first snooker programme *Pot Black* on 23 July 1969 from the BBC Studios in Birmingham. This was at a time when the BBC began broadcasting in colour, and were looking for programmes that could benefit from the new technology. Ray Reardon beat John Spencer in the first final.

TOP TWENTY UNUSUAL SOUNDING BIRMINGHAM BANDS

Ricky Cool & the Icebergs
Brent Ford and the Nylons
Napalm Death
El Riot and the Rebels
The Idle Race
Tea & Symphony
Pat Wayne and the Beachcombers
The Honeydrippers
2 Men, a Drum Machine & a Trumpet
Ocean Colour Scene
The Mood Elevators
We've Got A Fuzzbox and We're Gonna Use It
Johnny West and the Sunsets
The Redbeards From Texas
Ned's Atomic Dustbin
Rory Storm and The Hurricanes
The Ugly's
Williams Conquerors
Wellington Kitch Jump Band
Al Jackson & the Jaguars

ORIGINS OF BANDS

The band Duran Duran will forever be associated Broad Street. The members were Nick Rhodes (keyboards), John Taylor (bass guitar), Roger Taylor (drums), Andy Taylor (guitar) and Simon Le Bon on vocals. The name Duran Duran came from a character called Dr Durand Durand in the film *Barbarella*. Barbarella was at the time of the band's formation a club near the Rum Runner in Broad Street.

Dexys Midnight Runners were formed in 1978 and played at the Barrel Organ pub. 'Come On Eileen' reached number 1 in August 1982. Kevin Rowland and Kevin Archer are said to have named the band after Dexedrine, a recreational drug, although the band was anti-drugs!

Fairport Convention have been one of the most well-known folk rock groups since 1967. They met, or convened, for rehearsals at a house named Fairport, the family home of rhythm guitarist Simon Nicol.

Black Sabbath started in Birmingham in the late 1960s and was originally called Earth, but changed their name and became a highly successful heavy metal band – *Black Sabbath* was one of Boris Karloff's horror movies. Their album *Paranoid* topped the album charts in October 1970.

Traffic was named by band member Jim Capaldi who came up with the name while watching cars clog a street following a show. As a result a band already called 'Traffic Jam' renamed themselves Status Quo!

Chicken Shack with 'I'd Rather Go Blind' reached number 14 in May 1969. Lead female vocalist, Christine Vie (née Perfect), was born in Cumbria but moved to Bearwood as her father became a concert violinist and music lecturer at St Peter's College in Saltley. It is said that her grandfather was a one-time organist at Westminster Abbey. Chicken Shack were named after a Jimmy Smith record 'Back at the Chicken Shack'. Chicken Shacks were popular American chicken restaurants at the time.

Heavy metal band Judas Priest formed in 1968 with Rob Halford, Glenn Tipton and Ian Hill. They have sold over 45 million albums. The band got its name from the Bob Dylan song 'The Ballad of Frankie Lee and Judas Priest'. It is said that Judas Priest was originally a mild curse said to avoid saying 'Jesus Christ'.

Fine Young Cannibals took their name after the 1960 movie *All The Fine Young Cannibals* with Robert Wagner, a film which, presumably the band members, David Steele, Roland Gift and Andy Cox, liked. They are best known for their 1989 hit single 'She Drives Me Crazy'.

UB40 are a popular reggae and ska band that formed in 1978 and were named after the Social Security form for claiming unemployment benefit.

Led Zeppelin was so named after singer shared a joke about forming a band that they said would 'go down like a lead balloon'. Later they chose the name Lead Zeppelin, but are said to have dropped the 'a' so that Americans wouldn't mispronounce it. Led Zeppelin's first live gig was at Surrey University in October 1967.

The Move, with Roy Wood, Carl Wayne and Bev Bevan, joined forces at the Cedar Club on Constitution Hill. Their 1967 hit 'Flowers in the Rain' was the first record played on BBC Radio One. The group's members had all been in other bands and the name refers to the move various members made to form the group.

The Moody Blues have sold 70 million albums worldwide and have been awarded 14 platinum and gold discs, a far cry from 1964 when they were called 'The MBs'. It is thought they were after sponsorship from M&B brewery, but they became the Moody Blues owing to their interest in Duke Ellington, a performer who had a song called 'Mood Indigo' and they liked mood-changing music.

The Flower Pot Men had a hit in 1967 with 'Let's Go To San Francisco'. The band members apparently liked the children's TV programme *Bill & Ben the Flower Pot Men* and it has been suggested the word pot relates to the slang term for cannabis, popular at the time the band went to the top of the pots, er, pops, in the height of the flower power era.

The Ivy League, formed by Small Heath-born John Carter and Ken Lewis, with friend Perry Ford, reached number 3 in the Hit Parade with 'Tossing and Turning' in 1965. They took their name from their smart appearance. The fashion at the time was for smart jackets and haircuts, the jackets were known in the fashion world as ivy leagues.

Ned's Atomic Dustbin took their name from an episode of the *Goon Show*. Their hit EP had a suitable sounding name, *Kill Your Television*, and they signed with Birmingham-based indie label Chapter 22 Records.

The Rockin' Berries reached number 3 with 'He's in Town' in October 1964 and no. 5 with 'Poor Man's Son' a year later. Five of the band – Roy Austin, Clive Lea, Geoff Turton, Terry Bond and Chuck Botfield – were from Birmingham. The group was originally called The Bobcats and later the Rockin' Berries simply because they played a lot of Chuck Berry songs.

The Brumbeats were originally called The Plazents, named in honour of the Plaza Ballroom in Old Hill where the band became the resident act.

THE BEATLES

The Beatles played five dates in Birmingham:

10 March 1963: Hippodrome Theatre with Montez and Roe.
4 June 1963: Town Hall with Roy Orbison and Gerry and
The Pacemakers.
10 November 1963: Beatles top the bill at the Hippodrome with
The Kestrels and Peter Jay.
11 October 1964: Odeon with Mary Wells.
9 December 1965: Odeon with Moody Blues, The Paramounts and
The Koobas.

MUSICAL NOTES

Edna Iles, a classical pianist born in Kings Heath, played at concerts
all over the world. She had lessons from Appleby Matthews, the first
conductor of the City of Birmingham Orchestra. She died in February
2003 aged ninety-seven.

On 26 August 1846, the great feature of the Birmingham Musical Festival was Mendelssohn's new work of 'Elijah' with the composer himself present to conduct it. 'The nobility and gentry within a circle of fifty miles' were in attendance.

Yodelling superstar Frank Ifield was born in Coventry, brought up in Australia, but lived in Brum. His record 'I Remember You' was a major hit.

The Spencer Davis Group had hits with 'Keep on Running', 'Somebody Help Me', 'Gimme Some Lovin'' and 'I'm A Man'.

The first man from Birmingham to reach number 1 in the Hit Parade was Jimmy Jones in 1960 . . . but he was from Birmingham, Alabama.

The Applejacks became the first local group to make a big impact on the national music scene when they reached number 7 with 'Tell Me When' in March 1964. They were unusual for having a female guitarist Megan Davies. Band members Al Jackson and Phil Cash were both Brummies and Don Gould and Gerry Freeman were from Solihull.

The Fortunes with 'You've Got Your Troubles' reached number 2 in 1965 and they had three other top ten hits. They were formed in Brum and two members of the early band, Barry Pritchard, a guitarist, and Andy Brown who was the drummer, are from the city.

Electric Light Orchestra was a successful rock music group from the 1970s and '80s. Roy Wood, Jeff Lynne, and Bev Bevan formed the band in 1971.

Birmingham hosted the Eurovision Song Contest at the National Indoor Arena in May 1998.

SIX MUSICAL VENUES

The Ritz, Handsworth
The Rum Runner, Broad Street
The Morgue, Bearwood
The Cedar Club, Hockley
The Mother's Club, Erdington
The Golden Eagle, city centre

BIRMINGHAM'S SEVEN CITY ORGANISTS

Thomas Munden 1834–7
George Hollins 1837–41
James Stimpson 1842–6
C.W. Perkins 1888–1923
G.D. Cunningham 1924–48
George Thalben Ball 1948–83
Thomas Trotter 1983–present

READ ALL ABOUT IT!

Arthur Henry Sarsfield Ward was born in Ladywood in 1883 and became better known as Sax Rohmer who brought the mysteries of the Far East to his readership through his Fu Manchu stories.

Birmingham's Chief Police Constable from 1935 to 1941, Cecil Moriarty, wrote a book that is used all around the world, called *Moriarty's Police Law*. Presumably it can be bought for a few coppers.

J.H. Shorthouse (1834–1903), author of the Victorian best seller *John Inglesant*, an historical novel published in 1881, lived in Beaufort Road, Ladywood. His house was called Inglesant. His initials stand for Joseph Henry, although he was always known by his initials.

The Revd Wilbert Awdry devised the Thomas the Tank Engine stories during the Second World War when his son, Christopher, was ill in bed with measles. Awdry was a curate in Kings Norton at the time. The first book, *The Three Railway Engines* was published in 1945, and by the time Awdry stopped writing in 1972, the Railway Series numbered twenty-six books. Christopher subsequently added further books to the series.

Bill Oddie did much of his early birdwatching at Bartley Green Reservoir and his first ever published article, for the West Midland Bird Club's annual report, was about the birds of the reservoir.

Gavin Lyall who passed away in 2003 wrote top thriller stories *The Secret Servant* and *The Crocus List*. He married *Observer* columnist Katherine Whitehorn in 1958. His novel *Midnight Plus One* was made into a film starring Steve McQueen.

Dame Barbara Cartland, born in Edgbaston in 1901, became well known for her romantic novels and her trademark pink outfits.

Edgar Guest was more well known in the USA than his hometown of Birmingham, UK. From his first published work in the *Detroit Free Press* until his death in 1959, Guest penned some 11,000 poems which were syndicated in over 300 newspapers and collected in more than 20 books. He was made Poet Laureate of Michigan.

Thomas Aris set up a weekly newspaper, *Aris's Gazette*, in 1741 reporting on national and local events. It became a daily paper in 1862 and became known as the *Gazette* and eventually the *Birmingham Gazette*.

William Hutton ran away from his father's business in Nottingham and arrived in Birmingham where he set up in the book trade. He began researching the history of the town, eventually producing 75 copies of a book that explored Birmingham's history, and in so doing became Brum's first recorded historian.

Rip van Winkle was written in Birmingham in 1816, while the author Washington Irving was staying with his sister, Mrs Henry van Wart. Irving Street and Washington Street in Lee Bank were named in his honour.

In the late nineteenth century, poet and philosopher Constance Naden (1858–89) became a celebrated literary figure. Oscar Wilde, who was editing *Women's World* magazine, asked her to write a poem that appeared in the March 1888 issue.

4,000 people paid 6d each to see Charles Dickens read *A Christmas Carol* in the Town Hall on December 1853. The proceeds went to help pay for the Birmingham & Midland Institute.

Birmingham's biggest bookshop opened in a converted bank for Dillon's, now Waterstone's, on New Street.

Author Jim Grace studied English at Birmingham University before going to write his first novel *Continent* in 1986, which won the Whitbread First Novel prize. He is now an established author and his novel *Arcadia* is about a fictional city that is said to be loosely based on Birmingham.

SHAKESPEARE LIBRARY

The Shakespeare Library was established at a breakfast held by the lord mayor in April 1864 to celebrate the 300th anniversary of Shakespeare's birth when a collection of books and money was handed over to the town's library and a new room was completed for the exclusive storage of the Shakespeare collection. This was opened on 23 April 1868. A fire destroyed most of the Central Library in 1879 and only 500 out of 7,000 books from the Shakespeare Library were saved. The building was restored by June 1882.

BOOKS ABOUT BIRMINGHAM

Francis Brett Young was born in nearby Halesowen and used Birmingham settings in his novels *Cold Harbour*, *The House Under The Water*, *White Ladies* and *Undergrowth*.

Washington Irving's *Bracebridge Hall* was based on Aston Hall.

O.H. Davies of Small Heath based his novel *The Great City* on Birmingham.

Local coffee shop owner Andre Drucker wrote *Little Men in a Blind Alley*.

SEVEN PLACES TO SEE ON THE TOLKIEN TRAIL

Author J.R.R. Tolkien was born in South Africa in 1892, moving to Birmingham when he was three years old. He later wrote *The Hobbit* that was published in 1937 and *The Lord of the Rings* trilogy in 1954–5. Many of the places and buildings that are mentioned in his books are based on places he saw in Brum when he was growing up. He died in September 1973 leaving behind a mass of fantasy literature, although he only lived in Brum for sixteen years, living in eight different houses.

Oratory Church on Hagley Road. Mabel Tolkien's search for a sympathetic church took her to the Oratory in 1902. They lived nearby and J.R.R. attended St Philip's School adjacent to the church.

Perrott's Folly and Waterworks Tower. These two structures in Ladywood are said to have been the inspiration for Tolkien's 'Two Towers of Gondor' – 'Minas Tirith' and 'Minas Morgul'.

The Plough & Harrow Hotel on Hagley Road has two plaques related to Tolkien, one of which is in a bedroom where J.R.R. and his wife Edith stayed on the night before he joined up with the Lancashire Fusiliers in the First World War.

Moseley Bog. This was once a mill pool, a place of childhood adventures, and the inspiration for the 'Old Forest' where Tolkien's character Tom Bombadil lived.

Sarehole Mill. This is an eighteenth-century corn mill described by Tolkien as a 'kind of lost paradise'. When it fell into disuse Tolkien contributed to its restoration fund.

Tolkien lived for a while in Duchess Road, Ladywood. It was there that he met and fell in love with Edith Bratt, who was later to become his wife, although he was only sixteen when he met her.

IN THE LIBRARY

The Central Library was the largest in Europe at the time it opened in 1973, with 31 miles of shelving and 1,500,000 books. There are currently over 500,000 people who are members of the city's libraries and 221,724 members are actively using their tickets. Almost 5 million books are issued each year. At the last count there were 2,752,770 to choose from.

The current Central Library was officially opened by the then Prime Minister Harold Wilson in January 1974.

The oldest book in the library is *Catholicon* by Johannes Balbus, printed in Germany in 1469.

The oldest book printed in England in the Central Library is *Cordiale* or *Four Last Thinges*, printed by William Caxton 1479.

The smallest book is in the Bijou series, printed in about 1850, which is an inch tall.

The largest book in Birmingham Central Library is *Birds of America, 1827–1838*, 99cm by 66cm unopened, by John James Audubon.

The heaviest book in the Central Library is *Investigations and Studies in Jade*, the Heber R. Bishop Collection, 1906. The two volumes weigh 125lb.

AT THE FLICKS

The Oak Cinema at Selly Oak was once awarded a silver medal after being voted the second cleanest cinema in the country in July 1951.

Oscar Deutsch, born in Balsall Heath in 1893, opened his first venue in Perry Barr on 4 August 1930, and decided to call it the Odeon. It is widely believed that Odeon stands for 'Oscar Deutsch Entertains Our Nation'.

The first purpose-built cinema is said to have been the Picture Palace built in July 1910 on Lozells Road. By 1914 there were at least 46 different venues showing movies.

The Electric Theatre, which opened three weeks after the Picture Palace, was the first cinema in the city centre.

Film star Anne Heywood, from Handsworth, real name Violet Pretty, was once an usherette at the Palace Picture House in Erdington. She was Miss Great Britain in 1949.

3ft 8in Brum-born actor Kenny Baker played R2-D2 in *Star Wars*.

Birmingham's 25-acre Star City complex was the biggest leisure park in Europe at the time of its opening in 2000. The thirty-screen cinema was the largest in Europe.

The Futurist opened in July 1919. Al Johnson's *The Singing Fool* ran for two months non-stop in 1929, a record that survived until 1940 when *Gone With The Wind* blew in for sixteen weeks.

Broadway Plaza, a twelve-screen multiplex at Five Ways built on the site of the former Children's Hospital, opened in October 2003.

I'LL DRINK TO THAT

William Butler of Mitchells & Butlers beer fame came to Birmingham from Leicestershire and gained employment in a hairdressers. He married the daughter of the man who ran the Crown pub on Broad Street and eventually took charge at the pub. In so doing he moved from the crown of the head to head of the Crown.

Famous Brum brewers Ansells were based in Aston, partly on the former grounds of Aston Hall, and taking as their logo a squirrel. This was on the crest of Thomas Holte who owned Aston Hall. The home end at Aston Villa's ground is called the Holte End.

The Swan at Yardley was the biggest pub in Britain, with eight bars and ninety staff.

The Golden Lion was moved lock, stock and beer barrels from Digbeth to Cannon Hill Park in 1911.

The Dragon Inn on Hurst Street forms part of Birmingham's Chinese Quarter and takes its name from the highly popular dragon dance, a traditional Chinese dance performed on special occasions, particularly during Chinese New Year. Dragons are an important part of Chinese culture, symbolising good fortune.

One hugely successful pub that didn't exist in real life it was the Barmaid's Arms – it featured on BBC Radio WM with Malcolm Stent in a lunchtime programme recorded in the studio with the soundtrack of a real pub atmosphere in the background. The sounds were recorded in a nearby pub, the Selly Park Tavern. A sound man had to

sit in the pub for two hours to record the sound – it must have been an awful assignment, but someone had to do it.

The Fox pub on Hurst Street had a mirrored globe that once hung in the Grand Savoy Hotel in New York.

The Malthouse pub on the canal side opposite Brindleyplace became famous in May 1998 when US President Bill Clinton dropped by for a pint while attending the G8 leaders' conference at the ICC. His security staff were rumoured to have smashed his empty glass, to stop souvenir hunters or people wanting his fingerprints or DNA from getting their hands on it. Less famously, actor Ken Morley, Reg Holdsworth of *Coronation Street* fame, opened the pub. I think it is safe to assume that is not the reason why Clinton dropped in for a pint.

In 1880 Birmingham had an amazing number of pubs including fifteen Red Lions and three Black Lions, fourteen White Swans, eleven Swans, and four Swans With Two Necks, two Dogs and two Dogs & Ducks as well as three Red Cows, four Beehives and two Eagles. There was no partridge in a pear tree, but there were six Dog & Partridges.

PUB NAMES TO DISCUSS OVER A DRINK OR TWO

The Why Not? pub, now demolished, may have been an encouragement for people to go in, but Why Not? was the name of the horse which won the 1894 Grand National, so it may have been named after the winning nag, and why not?

The Briar Rose on Bennetts Hill gets its name from a painting and stained-glass windows by Sir Edward Burne-Jones who was born in that street in 1833. The pub opened in the former Abbey National building in 1999.

A pub at Birmingham Airport is named Dragonfly after the first aircraft to land at the airport, then called Elmdon, a Western Airways DH.90 Dragonfly, in March 1939.

Pear Tree is in Kings Heath, a suburb that began as a village with a scattering of cottages around the Cross Guns Inn. Dating from the eighteenth century, the inn was also known as the Pear Tree, as one grew in front of the pub.

The Harriers on Broadway, Aston, was built near to the site of the track at the Lower Grounds athletic venue and two bars, the Blewitt Bar and Radford Bar, are named in honour of former athletes.

Bacchus Bar in Burlington Arcade is named after the Greek God of wine and fertility. It is located in the basement of the four-star Burlington Hotel on New Street.

The Tap & Spile on Gas Street dates back to 1821. A spile is a small wooden peg used to control the flow of air into, and carbon dioxide out of, a cask of ale.

The Barton Arms in Aston was built between 1899 and 1901. It was threatened with demolition in 1969. Two bars have snob screens, which survive in less than twenty pubs in the whole of the UK.

The Hornet at Ward End recalls Wolseley/Austin's Hornet car first produced in 1930 at a motor works that stood near the pub.

The Spitfire, Castle Bromwich, is built near to the former Castle Bromwich airfield which contained the largest Spitfire factory in the UK, building over half of the approximately 20,000 built.

Man on the Moon at West Heath was called Man in the Moon until Neil Armstrong took one small step for man in July 1969.

The Bottle of Sack in Sutton Coldfield. The name of this pub comes from a quote in Shakespeare's play *Henry IV*, 'fill me a bottle of sack: our soldiers shall march through; we'll to Sutton Co'fil' tonight.' Shakespeare's mother, Mary Arden, was said to be a member of a leading local family.

PUBS NAMED AFTER PEOPLE

The Elizabeth of York in Moseley is near St Mary's Church. A local landmark for centuries, the church stands on land donated by Elizabeth of York, wife of King Henry VII.

The Soloman Cutler on Regency Wharf, Broad Street, stands mainly on the site of Pearce & Cutler's Glass Works, founded by Soloman Cutler, in 1854.

The Arthur Robertson is near the Perry Barr athletics track and the pub is named after Birchfield Harriers' most famous runner. At the 1908 Olympics, he won a gold medal in the 3-mile team race, in which he individually finished second, and he won a silver medal in the steeplechase.

The Charlie Hall in Erdington opened in May 2000. It takes its name from the actor who appeared in forty-seven films with Laurel and Hardy. Charlie Hall was born on 19 August 1899, in a small cottage nearby.

MAKING A MEAL OF THINGS

In 1837 Alfred Bird, a chemist, made a powder which enabled eggless custard to be made, so pleasing his wife who was allergic to eggs and also a baking powder which could be used to make bread without yeast. This was used by the troops in the Crimean War, enabling the men to have fresh bread on the frontline. Alf looked after the health of the nation!

Ernest Henry Wilson was a botanist who travelled the world collecting 100,000 species of plants and he introduced the Western World to the Kiwi fruit. A blue plaque was unveiled in his honour, in May 2010, at the Botanical Gardens where he trained in botany from 1893 to 1897.

Birmingham's foremost Chinese food man is Wing Yip who came to Birmingham from Hong Kong in 1970. His wholesale and distribution centre in Nechells is one of the largest of its kind in the country. In 1994 he was named the UK's leading Chinese entrepreneur in the annual Chinese Leadership Awards.

Typhoo Tea had premises at a canal side wharf in Digbeth where the tea tips were delivered and packed into packets from 1923 until 1941 when a German bomb rearranged the building. No doubt workers needed more than a cuppa. Tea was lasted packed there in 1987.

Birmingham was once famous for its annual onion fair, often held in the Serpentine Grounds which is approximately the current location of Aston Villa FC; so when people leave Villa Park with tears in their eyes it may be because they can still smell and breathe in the onions rather than a reflection on the standard of football.

In 1782, fifty-six wagon loads of onions were on sale at the onion fair. By 1875 the council official in charge, clearly a man who knew his onions, decided that the fairs led to 'drunkenness and fighting, and were demoralising and vulgar'

and no council land should be used for onion stalls. No doubt this led to a lot of crying, but the fair survived in various forms until the early 1960s and was briefly revived at Brindleyplace in September 1992.

Bananas were imported, ripened and stored under the arches of the viaduct in Allison Street, Digbeth, and at the Geest warehouse that dates back to 1840.

TEN BALTI BELT FOODSTUFFS AND HOW TO COOK THEM

Arabi: used like a potato, peel and boil.

Chora: top and tail, cook like a green bean.

Duddi: top and tail, peel, slice and fry.

Karela: deseed, top and tail and boil.

Mooli: peel and boil or raw in salads, like a turnip.

Okra: steam and cook with potatoes.

Rivya: small aubergines, top, tail slice and fry.

Tinda: like Okra use with chicken.

Toreya: top, tail, peel, chop and fry, sweetish taste.

Valor: tastes like green beans.

TWENTY BALTI-SPEAK WORDS TO GET YOUR TEETH INTO

Aloo: potato.

Balti: flat-bottomed wok, or pan, used to cook the food.

Bhaji: deep fried onion fritters.

Chapati: sometimes called roti, this is a flour and water mixed pancake-shaped bread.

Dal: dried lentils and pulses.

Dip: yoghurt and mint or chutney mixed with onions, usually served on arrival at the balti house.

Dhansak: hot and sweet dish with lentils and tomatoes.

Gosht: lamb.

Kofta: spicy meatball.

Korma: a Balti with nuts and cream.

Lassi: yoghurt drink, slated or seasoned.

Masala: Balti with cream, almonds and extra spices.

Murghi: Kashmiri chicken.

Naan: bread with special flour, yeast, eggs, milk and sugar.

Pakora: potatoes, onions, flour, spices deep fried.

Papadum: very thin and crispy round accompaniment to the meal

Saag: spinach.

Tandoor: clay charcoal oven used for baking.

Tikka: chicken or lamb marinated in yoghurt and cooked on a skewer.

7

STREETS & ROADS

TEN STREETS NAMED AFTER PEOPLE

Aberdeen Street isn't named after the Scottish city but after Lord Aberdeen, the Prime Minister, who declared the Crimean War against Russia in 1854. It was around that time the street was built.

Rickman Drive, Lee Bank, is named after a well-known architect, Thomas Rickman who designed numerous churches including the nearby St Thomas' Church on Bath Row. He was also co-designer of the Midland Bank on Waterloo Street.

Greenwood Place, Kingstanding, contains the 30,000th municipal house in Birmingham and is named after the man who opened it in 1932, Mr A. Greenwood, the Minister of Health.

Brays Road off Barrows Road near the airport commemorates Thomas Bray, Rector of Sheldon, who founded the Missionary Society for the Propagation of the Gospel in 1700.

Carless Avenue in Harborne has, sadly, no link with people who don't drive but is instead named after the Carless family who lived in the area from at least the 1530s.

John Bright Street was named after the town's MP of over 30 years' standing (and no doubt occasionally sitting!). It was cut in 1881.

Marshall Street is near Blucher Street and they both commemorate the Prussian who fought alongside the Duke of Wellington at Waterloo.

Part of the Northfield relief road opened in 2007 is called Isaac Tongue Junction, named in honour of a local blacksmith. He was well known for christening babies with nicknames over his anvil after their official baptisms had taken place.

Holliday Street was named after the Mayor of Birmingham 1863–4, William Holliday.

A road at the Queen Elizabeth Hospital is called Vincent Drive, in honour of Sir Harry Vincent who gave money towards the building of the hospital. Harry made his fortune in confectionery and established the famous Blue Bird toffee factory at Hunnington not far from Halesowen in 1925.

KEEP IT IN THE FAMILY

Numerous roads on the Calthorpe Estate are named after members of the family and their connections. Gough Road is from the Gough family, who owned much of the area from 1717. Calthorpe Road is named after the Calthorpes of Elvetham in Hampshire, hence Elvetham Road.

Barwick Street is named after William Barwick Cregoe Colmore, the last of the Colmore family.

Colmore Row is named after the Colmore family.

Cornwall Street is named after the county where the Cregoe family lived.

Eden Place next to the Council House was named after a daughter of Dr Thomas Eden, who married one of the Colmores.

Edmund Street was once called Harlow Street, but renamed after family member Edmund.

Margaret Street was named after Margaret Radcliffe, sister of William Barwick Cregoe Colmore in 1885.

Other streets named after the Colmore family include Henrietta Street, Charlotte Street and Lionel Street.

STREETS WITH INTERESTING ORIGINS

Livery Street is thought to be named after a riding school, Swann's Riding Academy, that was stabled there in the 1740s.

City Road was so called because it was started in 1889, the year that the town of Birmingham became a city. It was chosen to receive the name owing to the fact that of all the roads built that year, this was the longest at 1½ miles. It was also one of the first to be lined with trees.

Swallow Street was near Summer Street off Navigation Street; sounds nice, but the swallows were not of the feathered variety but were local landowners in the mid-eighteenth century.

Carrs Lane was once Goddes Carte Lane named after the processional cart belonging to St Martin's Church, which was used to carry the crucifix during the Whit procession.

Gas Street was the home of Birmingham's first gas works where Mr Gostling caused a bit of a stink by setting up the Birmingham Gas Light and Coke Company in about 1819.

Dogpool Lane, Stirchley, is probably a corruption of dockpool where lilies (or docks, as they were known) grew.

Electric Avenue, Aston, was named after the local factory the General Electric Company.

Raddlebarn Road, Selly Oak, takes its name from Raddlebarn Farm – raddle being a name for red ochre, which was used for marking sheep.

Great Stone Road, Northfield, is named after a glacial boulder from the Ice Age which formed the huge corner stone of the road.

Masshouse Circus/Lane was called after the church of St Mary Magdalen which stood nearby.

Gospel Lane, Acocks Green, derives from an oak tree on the parish boundary where locals met to read gospels from the Bible at Whitsun.

Hob Moor Road, Small Heath, is said to be the place where hobgoblins lived! These supernatural beings apparently inhabited local woods and hedgerows.

Monument Road, Ladywood, gets its name from a local folly or monument built by the Perrott family in 1758. There are a number of theories as to why it was built, including the ideas that the owner could spy on his ladylove from the top, or to spot deer!

Steelhouse Lane is, apparently, named after buildings called steelhouses that were used for iron making in the 1790s.

Moor Street is a corruption of Mole Street, which in turn is a corruption of Molendum, which meant mill.

SIX QUINTON ROADS
NAMED AFTER INVENTORS

In Quinton a series of neighbouring roads were named after inventors:

Hansom Road: Named after Joseph Hansom, designer of the Hansom cab.

Arkwright Road: In honour of Richard Arkwright of spinning fame.

Pitman Road: Named after Isaac Pitman of shorthand writing.

Wedgwood Road: Recalls the potter Josiah.

Faraday Road: In honour of Michael Faraday, the electrical bright spark.

Fleming Road: Alexander Fleming of penicillin fame.

WHO LIVED HERE?

Ozzy Osbourne the Black Sabbath rock star lived at 14 Lodge Road, Aston.

Author J.R.R. Tolkien made a 'hobbit' of moving addresses, but 4 Highfield Road was his last address in Birmingham.

Tony Hancock lived at 41 Southam Road, Hall Green, in May 1924. He lived there for more than half an hour.

J.S. Shorthouse, author of best-selling Victorian novel *John Inglesant*, lived at 6 Beaufort Road, Ladywood.

Samuel Lloyd lived at 13 Old Square; he founded Lloyd's Bank.

The first Mayor of Birmingham, William Schofield, lived at 1 Old Square.

Jeff Lynne of the Electric Light Orchestra lived at 368 Shard End Crescent, Shard End.

Politician Enoch Powell was born at Flaxley Lane, Stechford, in 1912.

MURALS, TIME CAPSULES, PLAQUES & WHERE TO FIND THEM

In January 1983 the lord mayor, Cllr Hollingworth, unveiled a small plaque in the middle of Five Ways island to commemorate the centenary of the opening of King Edward VI Grammar School on the site. The school moved to Bartley Green in 1958.

When the queen performed the opening ceremony of the International Convention Centre in June 1991 she unveiled a huge slate commemorative plaque which was carved from the Aberllefenni Quarry at Corris near Machynlleth. Ieuan Rees chiselled the lettering at his studios in Ammanford, Dyfed.

Marine life enthusiast fourteen-year-old Anna Seward buried the time capsule beneath the National Sealife Centre in Brindleyplace in May 1995. It contained newspaper cuttings about the £5 million centre, a sketch of the design signed by architect Sir Norman Foster and photos of Anna and her own home aquarium. It was made of the same clear acrylic used in the sealife tunnel, although no-one can actually look into its present location!

During the renovations to a Baptist Church in Kings Heath in January 2009 workmen uncovered a pottery container containing papers from 1872. These related to the beginning of Baptist worship in Kings Heath that began in 1811. Later the same workmen uncovered another container, that held more papers and a silver Queen Victoria Diamond Jubilee medal all dated 1897.

A girl climbing down a ladder into her lover's arms is on the bronze mural in Old Square depicting the elopement of the daughter of banker Sampson Lloyd III.

The boar's head on the weather vane on Birmingham Cathedral was the crest of Sir Richard Gough who persuaded George I to give £600 towards building the church.

The underpass mural at Holloway Head, which may look like a series of gaudy-coloured panels, actually depicts a city skyline leading into the city and a rural scene on the side leading out.

A huge mosaic, constructed in 1964, portrayed the role of Birmingham in the Civil War in arming the Roundheads and Cavaliers. It was in Old Square but was removed and not replaced in the recent redevelopment.

The city's Irish community erected a mural to John F. Kennedy and the Irish ambassador unveiled it in 1968. It was removed in recent years when the area around it was landscaped, and it is currently in quite a few pieces, awaiting a new home in the Irish Quarter.

A mosaic mural near Snow Hill station in St Chad's Circus, completed in 1969, was one of the largest murals in the country measuring 300ft by 17ft. It depicted the Great Western Railway's route from Snow Hill to London. Sadly it was removed to make way for road improvements.

Kenneth Budd constructed the Horse Fair mosaic in 1966 showing horse dealings in the area in 1908. Horse fairs date back to 1215 and were held in that *neigh*bourhood until 1911.

Members of the Lunar Society are remembered in carved sandstone memorials called Moonstones in Great Barr. They are: Josiah Wedgwood, Erasmus Darwin, Samuel Galton, William Murdoch, Matthew Boulton, James Watt, Joseph Priestley, James Keir and William Withering.

STATUES

A statue of comedian Tony Hancock, complete with trademark Homburg hat, looks gloomily along Corporation Street. The Brum-born comedian's statue is head and shoulders above the rest, being 12ft high. It stands near the Birmingham Blood Transfusion Service which is fitting as one of his most famous episodes was called *The Blood Donor*. The statue was unveiled by Sir Harry Secombe on 13 May 1996.

The Archbishop of Canterbury unveiled the statue of Bishop Gore (1853–1932) in St Philip's churchyard. He is depicted in his convocation robes with his right hand upraised in the act of bestowing the Episcopal blessing, and in his left hand is the pastoral staff. Gore was the first Bishop of Birmingham.

Thomas Attwood was one of Birmingham's first members of parliament and his reclining statue was unveiled in Chamberlain Square in January 1993. Priscilla Mitchell, Attwood's great-great-granddaughter, funded it. Attwood can be found reclining on the steps outside the Central Library. At the time of its construction there were calls for a bleeper to be fitted to it that it would go off if anyone was about to trip over it.

Nelson's statue in the Bullring was the first in the country to be erected in his honour. It was unveiled in 1809.

The unveiling of the Joseph Priestley statue in Council House Square, on 1 August 1874 was exactly 100 years to the day of Preistley's discovery of 'dephlogisticated air', which the statue depicts.

The most well-known piece of public art of the 1970s was the sensational statue of King Kong that stood in the gardens at the Bullring. You couldn't really miss it, as it was 22ft high, made of fibreglass and weighed 12cwt. He was sold off and became a large advert for the King Kong Kar Kompany before being taken to Edinburgh and it is currently in Penrith. Ape-parently a campaign is currently underway to bring him back home to where he maybe ape-reciated.

A 6ft-long nude bronze statue, which personified youth and vigour in Greek mythology, was commissioned to commemorate the start of the inner ring road in 1957. It was located at the Holloway Circus roundabout on the ring road until being stolen. It was recovered in 2002 and relocated across the city. The name, Hebe, was chosen following a competition in the *Birmingham Evening Mail*.

In 1987 twelve life-size flat bronze horses were erected alongside the mane, er, main, Birmingham to Wolverhampton railway. It was part of a scheme called Track Art and the first horse was unveiled by racing commentator Lord John Oaksey. They give the impression of iron horses galloping alongside the trains, which were once themselves known as iron horses and certainly brighten up the approach to Wolverhampton!

The South African War Memorial in Cannon Hill Park is by Albert Toft and commemorates the dead of the South African Campaign 1899–1902. It was erected at the instigation of the *Birmingham Mail*, paid for by public subscription and unveiled on 23 January 1906.

WORKS OF ART AROUND THE INTERNATIONAL CONVENTION CENTRE

In 1991 this area was the largest art project in Europe with 1 per cent of the building costs of the International Convention Centre being allocated for art works.

The now-demolished *Forward* statue by Raymond Mason was the main centrepiece of Centenary Square. It depicted the history of industry and people in the area and was made of fibreglass resin and polymer paint, but was sadly burned down in 2003 and not replaced.

Ron Haselden devised *Birdlife* in the ICC entrance canopy depicting multi-coloured neon birds in a tree which flashed on and off indicating movement and migration, and international travel to Birmingham, which is what the ICC is all about. Sadly, this hasn't operated for numerous years although human migration continues.

The bricks in Centenary Square are actually called paviors and there are 250,000 of them arranged in a Persian carpet design devised by Tess Jaray. In accordance with Persian tradition the pattern of the bricks contains a flaw that is difficult to detect.

David Patten produced a work of art depicting type punches that spell out the word 'Virgil'; this is nothing to do with *Thunderbirds* but it's to do with John Baskerville who lived nearby. It was he who invented the typeface that became known as Baskerville typeface. *Virgil* was a book of poems, the first to be produced in that new type of lettering.

The bronze fountain by Tom Lomax, *The Spirit of Enterprise*, showed the flow of time through the water movement with three great dishes representing commerce, industry and enterprise. It has been temporarily removed during construction of the new library.

Deanna Petherbridge designed the mural on the drum wall of Symphony Hall. It is 100ft across and stretches up for four levels.

The *History of Construction* by Vincent Woropay, near the box office at the ICC, begins with a plinth of four hydraulic props with Doric columns on top of them, topped off with a small hut-like framework of branches, all made of metal.

The huge glasswork over the quayside end of the ICC mall by Alex Beleschenko uses a combination of colours used in the city's pre-Raphaelite paintings.

The bronze 'cloud' on the quayside by Rod Tye, symbolises, er, well, no-one seems to know what, but it has 'come to rest in two pieces'. Other sculptures in the area were heavily criticised by the *Birmingham Evening Mail,* but this monstrosity wasn't. It was part-sponsored by *Mail*'s parent group.

The unveiling of the Boulton, Watt and Murdoch statue on Broad Street was held in September 1956. Guests on the day included Mrs Charis Thomas, a great-great-granddaughter of Matthew Boulton; Father Ivo Thomas & Col Patrick Thomas, both children of Mrs Charis Thomas, therefore great-great-great-grandsons of Boulton; Captain Andrew Gibson Watt, great-great-great-grandson of James Watt and Margaret Murdoch, great-great-niece of William Murdoch. Sir Percy Mills, chairman of W & T Avery, the current owners of the Soho Foundry that was established by Boulton in 1761, unveiled the statue to a great-great-great-great round of applause.

WORKS OF ART IN VICTORIA SQUARE

Victoria Square is not a square and never has been.

It was revamped at a cost of £3.2 million, partly funded by a grant from the Regional Development Fund and the Henry Moore Foundation. Community artist Dhruva Mistry designed the key works of art.

The land slopes 4.5 metres from the Council House down to New Street which made it an ideal location for a cascading fountain.

The fountain is one of the largest in any city centre in Europe, measuring 27 metres long, 18 metres wide across the top pool and 10 metres across the lower pool.

3,000 gallons of water per minute are pumped through the pool.

The pools were lit by around 4,000 metres of fibre optic lights that were replaced by more energy efficient coloured lights in 2010.

The centrepiece of the top pool is a giant female form known as *The River*, but more popularly known as *The Floozie in the Jacuzzi*, after a similar style of sculpture in Dublin. It was cast in bronze and weighs 1.75 tonnes and rises 3.5 metres above the water.

The top pool has a quotation from T.S. Eliot's 'Four Quartets':

> And the pool was filled with water out of sunlight
> And the lotus rose, quietly, quietly,
> The surface glittered out of heart of light,
> And they were behind us, reflected in the pool,
> Then a cloud passed, and the pool was empty.

The lower pool contains a stony-faced boy and girl, known collectively as *The Youth*. They sit on a cube and a cylinder with water spouting from three bronze bowls in the shape of a honeysuckle bloom.

Two large sphinx-like figures known as *The Guardians* sit at the entrance to the square, and stand 4 metres above the podium, each weighing around 30 tonnes. They are imaginary beings, 'symbolic protectors of civic pride and dignity', suggesting, apparently, 'agility, power, strength and reasoning which convey a sense of balance, harmony and peace' and provide something for the kids to climb on.

If laid end to end the paviors in Victoria Square would stretch for no less than 30 miles.

90 tonnes of Darley Dale sandstone was used for retaining walls and the planters. This is the same type of stone that was used to build the Council House a century earlier.

The oldest statue is that of Queen Victoria, unveiled on 11 January 1901 just eleven days before she died. At that time the square was actually called Council House Square and was renamed in honour of the late monarch on 7 February 1901. The statue is not the original 1901 version, which was made of marble and deteriorated owing to air pollution. In 1951 as part of the Festival of Britain celebrations it was recast in bronze and unveiled on 9 June 1951. Vicky was removed to a works in Telford and given a brush down to remove forty years of pigeon droppings. She was returned in time for the square's official reopening in 1993.

In February 2011 the statue received an addition, in the form of a sceptre which had been missing its top, known as a capital, since around 1990. The Victorian Society unearthed photographs of the original, which was used to recreate the missing object.

The Iron Man by Antony Gormley, Birmingham's most controversial statue, is on the edge of Victoria Square outside the former post office, later the TSB. The structure is a mummy-like man with feet underground and the whole things leans at an angle and is made of rusting iron. The TSB gifted the £100,000 statue to the people of Birmingham but 90 per cent of 1,200 callers in a telephone poll expressed their disapproval of the statue. It's not like a bank to upset anyone is it!

TEN STORIES WITH SOME FOUNDATION

The mayor, Joseph Chamberlain laid the corner stone of the Council House on 17 June 1874. To celebrate, he held a lunch in the Great Western Hotel and treated the public to a fireworks display in Aston Park.

The foundation stone of the Polish Millennium House, Digbeth, dates from September 1961. The centre is named after the Millennium of Christianity's arrival in Poland.

The foundation stone for Kent Street, Birmingham's first public baths, was laid in October 1849. The council splashed out £23,000 on the building which comprised 'sixty-nine private hot and cold water baths, three plunge baths and a public wash-house with a laundry fitted up with twenty-five washing stalls and two sets of seventeen drying horses and other appliances.'

The Earl of Dartmouth, acting for George III, laid the foundation stone of Christ Church in what became Victoria Square on 22 July 1805. It was the first church in Birmingham to have free seating for the public, but kept men and women separate. Demolition of the church, which once stood on the site of Victoria Square, started in January 1899.

Comedian Ken Dodd laid the foundation stone at the extension to the Birmingham Hippodrome Theatre in 1999 at the start of a £24 million redevelopment programme. The man from Knotty Ash was remembered for his performance in the pantomime *Humpty Dumpty* in 1965. It was obviously all it was cracked up to be because it gained the theatre its highest ever attendance.

On 17 December 1907, the foundation stone was laid for the new St Paul's Girls' School which was, at that time, being established in Edgbaston by the Sisters of Charity of St Paul. That stone was blessed by Archbishop Ilsley and exactly 100 years later, to the very day, a replacement foundation stone, a replica of the original, was blessed and laid by Archbishop Vincent Nichols.

A farmer, Robert Plant, from Sutton left a legacy of £1,000 to build a church on condition that the foundation stone was laid within seven years of his death. In July 1951, with just one day left, Archbishop Masterson laid the foundation stone at St Nicholas' Church, in Jockey Road, Sutton Coldfield. It was opened on 10 March 1953.

Singers Hill Synagogue in the city centre is Britain's oldest grade II listed daily working synagogue. The foundation stone was laid in April 1855 and it was opened a year later by the then Chief Rabbi Dr Nathan Adler. In 1871, during alterations to the building, the original foundation stone was discovered. A plaque attached to it listed the names of the five principal men of the congregation: David, son of Solomon; Judah, son of Coleman; Solomon, son of Mordecai; Jacob, son of Samuel and Moses, son of Lyon.

The ceremony to lay the foundation stone for the Birmingham Municipal Bank's new head offices in Broad Street took place on 22 October 1932. The branch was to close for business exactly sixty-six years later on 23 October 1998.

The foundation stone for the International Convention Centre was originally laid in October 1986 by Jacques Delors, president of the European Commission, and removed to its present location on the quayside in March 1991, where Cllr Pat Sever and Euro MP John Tomlinson unveiled it.

DIDN'T THIS USED TO BE . . .

The Birmingham & Midland Eye Hospital at the junction of Church Street and Edmund Street is now an office block.

The Gas Hall art and exhibition gallery in Edmund Street used to be where people went to pay their gas bills – it was known as the Gas Rates Hall.

Cadbury's first factory was just off Broad Street and in 1884 it became Bridge Street Technical School, set up by George Dixon. It is assumed the pupils didn't receive free chocolate.

Castle Vale estate was built from 1964 on an old aerodrome, the aim being to produce a town the size of Stratford in four years. This was accomplished on time with 20,000 people moving there mainly from the inner-city zone.

One of the city centre's oldest buildings, the NatWest bank on Bennetts Hill, which opened as the National Provincial Bank of England, is now a pub called Bennetts. It's a building in which you still hand over lots of money, but generally feel happier about it than you once did.

The former industrial area around Nechells Gas Works close to Spaghetti Junction was cleared and a 390,000sq ft leisure complex known as Star City was opened in 2000. It is said to contain Europe's largest multiplex cinema.

The Broadway Plaza entertainment complex at Five Ways was originally the Children's Hospital, the frontage was retained when a state-of-the-art twelve-screen cinema complex was opened in 2003 with numerous bars and restaurants.

The Mailbox mixed-use shopping, leisure and office complex gets its name from the fact that it was once the main postal sorting office. The sorting office moved to a new £40 million development in Newtown that got underway in January 1997. It was a red letter day for The Mailbox when it opened in 1998.

Waterstone's bookshop on New Street was once a branch of the Midland Bank but was transformed during a year-long restoration project in 1993. The grade II listed building dates back to 1865 and was originally taken over by Dillon's bookshops before becoming Waterstone's. With 100,000 books it is the largest bookshop outside London and probably the most beautiful. Someone should write a book about it.

An Aston mosque built in 1988 changed its name to Jame Masjid Mosque in 2003. Its original name was the President Saddam Hussein Mosque.

A magnificent Victorian building on Brindleyplace bears an 1877 datestone, although it opened as a primary school in January 1878 with 807 pupils. It later became the George Dixon Higher Grade School. In recent years it was redeveloped as the Ikon Gallery.

HOME FROM HOME

In 1926 a man and wife with three children could be accepted as 'good tenants' of a three-bedroom, non-parlour type house, only if the man had an income of 70s a week or more'.

Kingstanding, the largest 1930s development, had 5,000 municipal houses by 1939.

On 9 December 1930 the council heard of 'Birmingham's first real move against slum clearance' in a report which called for the demolition of 4,700 'slum dwellings'.

In 1935 the 10,000th council house was officially opened in Hopstone Road by the then Prime Minister Neville Chamberlain. This made Birmingham the first local authority in Britain to build 10,000 council properties, just 15 years after building its first.

The 10,000th postwar council house opened in 1952 at 58 Admington Road, Garretts Green. It had taken 5½ years to build the first 5,000, but only 18 months to erect the other 5,000. At that time 250,000 people were said to be living in overcrowded conditions.

A report produced in 1947 noted that Birmingham had 30,000 houses in need of repair, mostly built between 1830 and 1875.

In 1955 a deputation from Birmingham told the government that the city, 'had 30,000 Irish immigrants and 9,000 from the Colonies.'

In 1956 Birmingham Housing Department was responsible for 105,671 dwellings.

As Birmingham expanded the first overspill agreements were made in 1955 with Droitwich, Tamworth, Redditch and Daventry.

Birmingham built its first twelve-storey block of flats at Great Francis Street, Nechells, in 1954.

During the period 1945–70, 5,000 homes were demolished and 81,000 were built. The peak year was 1967 when 9,000 were erected.

Between 1966 and 1968 Brum built more houses than Liverpool, Manchester and Sheffield put together.

By 1970 there were still 26,000 houses which lacked hot water taps, and 28,000 had no fixed bath.

A survey in 1983 showed that nearly half of Birmingham's pre-1919 houses were structurally unsound, in bad repair or lacking basic amenities.

COMPREHENSIVE REDEVELOPMENT AREAS

Plans were drawn up for five new comprehensive redevelopment areas. These were:

Parts of Aston and Nechells: This was to be renamed Nechells Green but the name didn't catch on.

The Summer Lane area: This became known as Newtown.

Ladywood: This was the only one of the five areas to retain its name due to it being a 'pleasant sounding name' with 'rich historical association'.

The Bath Row area: This became Lee Bank, the names Churchill Rise or Great Chamberlain were rejected in favour of Lee Bank.

The Gooch Street area: This became known as Highgate. The names Calthorpe, Forest Island, Silver Vale, Rea Bourne and Belgravia were rejected.

THE ROTUNDA

Work began on the Rotunda's construction in March 1961. At that time it was described as a 'concrete-cored candle'.

The building had four clocks each 28ft by 8ft in size.

In May 1981 newsreader Angela Rippon switched on a 3,972sq ft advert for Coca-Cola which was the largest neon sign in the world, on the top of the building.

Planners wanted to demolish the Rotunda in the early 1990s and replace it with a Manhattan-style skyscraper, as part of a redevelopment plan for the whole Bullring, but the scheme was abandoned in 1994.

There was a plan for a halo of neon lights round every floor with a 40ft-high weather vane that would change colour according to the weather. These plans never materialised. In 1992 it was again suggested the building should be topped with neon lights and lasers, as part of a £3 million redevelopment plan, but again this didn't happen.

The Rotunda was eventually turned into apartments that became popular with people who do not like hovering in the corners.

THE COUNCIL HOUSE

Mayor Jesse Collings opened the Council House on 31 October 1879.

The Birmingham Flute Society and Birmingham Glee Union performed at the opening event.

Guildhall and Municipal Hall were alternative names put forward for the name of the building.

An extension was built in 1912 and 124 tenders were received for the design.

Sculptures on the portico, the arch-shaped stone over the main entrance, show Britannia rewarding Birmingham manufacturers.

A huge 50ft by 9ft chandelier hangs over the central staircase.

The dome conceals a ventilation system with 500 jet gas rings where warm air was forced up drawing in cooler air from below. The only other system of this kind is in Buxton Opera House.

An ornate ceremonial lift was installed in the foyer near the steps in 1909. This was for the infirm King Edward VII who visited the city to open Birmingham University.

In the council chamber behind where the lord mayor sits is a screen of Riga oak with panels of Italian walnut depicting Art and Industry.

The Mace is the civic symbol of authority. It was presented to the city by Elkington's to mark 60 years of Queen Victoria's reign.

The main banqueting suite is 160ft long and has five chandeliers. Rodney and Del Boy are not employed to do the repair works.

There are six pieces of civic silver kept in the Council House:

The Holte Dish: A dish engraved with the coat of arms of Sir Charles Holte of Aston Hall. Made in London, 1673.

The King's Cup: A goblet made in Birmingham in 1935 and used by the lord mayor to present the Loyal Toast at banquets.

The Sayer Cradle: presented to the Lord Mayor H. Sayer in 1907 after the birth of his son, later given by him to the city.

The Attwood Cup: Presented by the artisans of Birmingham to politician Thomas Attwood in 1814.

The Muntz Casket: presented to the second mayor, P. Muntz, made by Elkington's in 1888–9.

The Darwin Tureen: a silver tureen manufactured for Robert Darwin and his wife Susannah, daughter of Josiah Wedgwood. Purchased by the city in 1949.

THE INTERNATIONAL CONVENTION CENTRE

Design and build work took a total of 3,500 man-years.

100,000 cubic metres of excavations were carried out.

9,000 tonnes of steel and steel reinforcements were used.

There are a total of 28,000 square metres of suspended ceiling.

It contains 9 acres of carpet, equal to seven football pitches, or 186 tennis courts.

The kitchen contains around 70,000 pieces of cutlery, 68,000 items of crockery and 15,000 articles of linen.

It also contains 3,500 square metres of planar glass. The mall has 500 square metres of double-glazing.

Before the ICC was built the land use was as follows:

Transport use road, rail and canal	27.5 per cent 6.75ha
Vacant	26.5 per cent
Industrial	16.0 per cent
Car parks	12.5 per cent
Public buildings	8.5 per cent

Rest: commercial, entertainment and religious.

The first official public meeting held at the ICC was in Hall 4 for the local Civic Centre Residents' Association in September 1990, six months before the first paying convention.

The first conferences at the ICC

The first conference was that of the British Small Animal Veterinary Association which took place 4–7 April 1991. There were 2,600 delegates and 1,000 exhibitors and guests. The British Small Animal Veterinary Association has chosen to hold its annual congress at the International Convention Centre for the twentieth consecutive year.

Between 7–9 April 1991 Woolworths held their annual conference for 240 suppliers.

The English Tourist Board attracted 400 delegates representing all UK tourist authorities on 10 and 11 April 1991.

Ecotec attracted 150 delegates on 10–12 April 1991.

Also on 10 April 1991 there were events for 'Global Maths for Birmingham Project', 'Local Government and NHS Reforms', 'NM Financial Management' and the 'Birmingham Readers and Writers Festival'.

The Socialist Group on the European Parliament got together 250 delegates who used the simultaneous interpretation booths for the first time in Hall 1 for nine languages.

On 12 April 1991 Birmingham City Council Planning Department held a meeting there. Bet they'd been planning it for ages!

The next event, on 11 April 1991, seemed more interesting . . . it was a Golden Wedding Anniversary for a couple who had visited the ICC on the day it opened.

SYMPHONY HALL

Symphony Hall opened on 15 April 1991.

The acoustics, designed by Artec of New York, were at the time the most advanced in the world.

The hall was built on 2,000 rubber pads which act as shock absorbers to prevent vibration and the space between the blocks absorbs the noise of trains travelling through the nearby railway tunnel.

A computer programme was developed to design the optimum shape of the hall, which turned out to be like a traditional nineteenth-century Viennese concert hall.

Inside there is a huge acoustic canopy, reverberation chambers and acoustic banners.

The acoustic canopy can be lowered to 10 metres above the stage for a solo recital and 14 metres above for an orchestral concert. It weighs 35 tons and is balanced by a single 35-ton steel and concrete block behind the organ.

The reverberation chamber has twenty-two adjustable electronically operated doors that can be opened to allow sound to fill the void behind them creating a cathedral-like effect. When fully open the volume of the hall is increased by 50 per cent. It was the first of its kind in Europe.

There are 2,261 seats, including 200 choir seats behind the stage and 877 of which are on the main floor.

It took less than three years for Symphony Hall to play host to 1 million people.

Halls at the ICC

Hall 1 is the main conference hall with 1,500 permanent seats. Alternate rows can be turned into desks. There are twelve simultaneous interpretation booths. There is a 28-metre-high fly tower for raising/lowering displays. The stage is big enough to turn an articulated lorry on it.

Hall 2 is the name of the 2,200-seater Symphony Hall.

Hall 3 is the largest hall and is basically an empty flat-floored space used for exhibitions. It can hold 3,000 temporary seats. The roof beams are strong enough to suspend a huge lorry for display purposes.

Hall 4 is flat-floored hall often used for social events.

Halls 5, 6, 7 and 8 are mini versions of Hall 1 but can be merged into one larger complex with smaller breakout areas as required.

Halls 6, 7, 8, 9, 10 and 11 are small seminar rooms that can be subdivided.

Prince Charles saw a model of the Broad Street Redevelopment Area in November 1987 and likened the ICC to a 'concrete missile silo'. Cllr Pat Sever responded, 'Brummies tend to be brash. They like modern buildings.'

BRINDLEYPLACE

Brindleyplace is a major office and leisure area next to the ICC and when built it was the largest mixed-use development in the country.

It is named in honour of canal engineer James Brindley who was responsible for the canal that forms an edge to the development.

Throughout his life Brindley built 365 miles of canal, one for every day of the year, maybe he had a break on leap years!

No. 1 Brindleyplace was the only new office building to be completed in Birmingham in 1995.

The Brindleyplace car park claims to be 'one of the safest parking experiences in the city', and so it should be with 54 closed-circuit TV cameras monitoring it 24 hours a day!

The Brindleyplace Dragonboat Festival has been held for the last twelve years and in 2010 raised over £43,000 for charity.

The imaginatively titled 'The Water's Edge' development, an eating and drinking area on the water's edge, receives around 2 million people each year, spending up to £13.9 million.

No. 5 Brindleyplace is the regional headquarters of BT. During construction 13,000 cubic metres of earth was removed. Apparently it would have taken one man with a shovel 13½ years to finish it, lucky then that they employed more than one man and they used a few diggers as well.

The building contains 3,500 cubic metres of concrete, that's enough to fill 111,000 wheelbarrows.

It contains 300,000 bricks which, if stacked on top of each other, would reach a height of 75,000ft, twice the height of the cruising altitude of an airliner.

THE TOWN HALL

The Town Hall is not really a town hall at all as it doesn't contain the Council Chamber, Lord Mayor's parlour, or the offices of any politician.

The Town Hall was commissioned after a petition from the townspeople was read on 3 May 1828. The grade I listed building was built in 1834.

On 6 June 1831 it was announced that Joseph Hansom who also designed the Hansom Cab, had won a £100 competition to oversee the construction of the Town Hall.

When construction commenced, a kiln was created within the building to bake bricks made with clay from the foundation excavations.

Originally budgeted for £17,000, the construction bill totalled £25,000.

The stone known as Anglesey marble had to be shipped 80 miles by sea and 100 miles by canal to reach Birmingham from quarries in North Wales.

When it opened the organ was the biggest in the UK, and now with more than 6,000 pipes, it is still larger than most cathedral organs. Five leather bellows had to be hand pumped to draw in enough air to create the required pressure in the organ's pipes. These were replaced with hydraulic engines between 1888 and 1890.

The Town Hall was closed on health and safety grounds on 12 July 1996, although a special one-off last playing of the organ event was held in June 2004.

It eventually underwent a £35 million renovation before reopening in October 2007. £18.3 million came from the City Council, £13.7 million from the Heritage Lottery Fund and £3 million from the European Regional Development Fund.

It was restored to the single balcony design of 1834.

Town Hall events and happenings

The Town Hall's first event, in October 1834, was the Triennial Music Festival, held in aid of the Birmingham General Hospital.

At the premiere of *Elijah* on 26 August 1846, Mendelssohn received eight encores.

Charles Dickens performed three readings at Christmas 1853, one of which was *A Christmas Carol*.

It is said that the celebration of the election of Birmingham's first members of parliament brought the gallery balcony crashing to the floor.

Lloyd George escaped from the Town Hall after a riot in 1901 by disguising himself as a policeman and marched up Broad Street to Ladywood police station.

During the 1930s depression the Town Hall served as a centre for providing food to the children of the poor.

ASTON HALL

Sir Thomas Holte began to build Aston Hall in 1618 and took up residence in 1631, although it was not completed until 1635.

The Holte family lived in Aston for nearly 200 years.

By the middle of the fifteenth century the Holtes owned manors in Aston and Duddeston.

The home end of nearby Villa Park is known as the Holte End.

Many of the Holte tombs are in Aston parish church.

Thomas Holte was knighted in 1603.

In 1611 Sir Thomas was rich enough to buy the title of baronet. James I used the new baronet's money to raise an army and quell troubles in Ireland.

Royalist Holte saw his home besieged by Parliamentarians in 1643 and he appealed to the Governor of Dudley Castle for forty musketeers to help him defend the house.

There is a hole in the grand staircase where a cannon ball went through a window, an open door and into the banister.

Thomas Holte encouraged the iron industry by having a forge on the River Tame. He also had the old medieval fields enclosed.

Sir Thomas disinherited his eldest living son, Edward, for marrying the Bishop of London's daughter, Elizabeth King.

The house remained in the family until 1817 when it was sold and leased by James Watt Jnr, son of the world-famous industrial pioneer James Watt.

It was bought by the city in 1864 becoming the first historic country house to pass into municipal ownership.

SOHO HOUSE

Soho House, now a museum, was home to Matthew Boulton from 1766 to 1809.

Matty purchased a Bramah patent water closet for Soho House in 1787.

The main staircase has holes in the risers of the steps which allowed warm air to circulate into the building.

Boulton complained in 1796 that: 'the gravil walk is littered with horse dung and in wet weather . . . broke up and [is] totally unfit for Ladies with satin shoes to walk out on.'

Soho House was the home of Matthew Boulton for forty-three years. It has also been used as a vicarage, private house, girls' school, and a police hostel.

In 1990 Birmingham & Museum Art Gallery began to turn the clock back by restoring the building to how it looked in about 1790.

The front portico was demolished by a lorry in the wartime blackout and rebuilt in 1950.

Servants used a hidden door called a jebb to bring food quickly to the dining room.

A chair in Bolton's study is a mahogany Klismo chair dating from 1800. It is one of a pair, the other being in the Victoria & Albert Museum in London.

Soho House has a central heating system that dates from the 1790s. It is thought to be the first successful attempt to heat a large house by ducted hot air since Roman times.

THE ORIGINAL BULLRING SHOPPING CENTRE FACTS & FIGURES

The Bullring market was opened for trade on 14 November 1963.

The Duke of Edinburgh officially opened the centre in May 1964.

The shopping and market complex covered 4 acres.

160,000 cubic yards of earth had to be excavated.

1,500,000 bricks were laid.

3,000 tons of steel was used.

2 acres of glass was installed.

136 miles of scaffolding was erected.

33 miles of electric wiring was installed.

Workers drank 28,000,000 gallons of tea during the 2½-year construction period. The number of portaloos is not recorded.

65,000 tonnes of concrete was removed from the old site.

12,000 tonnes of steel was taken for recycling.

THE NEW BULLRING
SHOPPING CENTRE FACTS & FIGURES

The new Bullring £550 million complex opened on 4 September 2003.

There are 150 shops on a 26-acre site.

Two buildings are suspended over a road and railway tunnel with four 120-tonne, 50-metre-long steel bowstring trusses.

During construction 216,000 tonnes of concrete was used.

15,460 tonnes of structural steelwork was used, twice the amount used to build the Eiffel Tower.

In the first full week of trading the centre received 1,169,122 visitors.

The new Bullring had its 4 millionth visitor less than four weeks after it opened.

Saturday is the busiest day of trading averaging 250,000 shoppers per day.

Sunday is now a busy day and 140,000 shoppers use the centre on the Sabbath.

In the first month 11.4 million pages were viewed on the Bullring's website.

Selfridges store is a £40 million structure clad with 15,000 shiny aluminium discs. The local paper suggested a number of nicknames: The Beehive, Glitterball, Fly's Eye and Crystal Tower, but locals just call it, er, Selfridges!

TWELVE INTERESTING BUILDINGS

The Free Libraries and Museums Act of 1850 gave the council the power to levy funding for the Museum and Art Gallery from the rates. Two gifts were offered to the town, and acted as incentive to carry through the scheme. These were a 7ft-high copper Buddha from about AD 400 offered by former mayor Samuel Thornton and a painting purchased by wellwishers entitled 'Dead Game' by local artist, Edward Coleman.

Millennium Point replaced the science museum. It's the size of six football pitches and it used enough block paving to build a path from Birmingham to Portsmouth.

The City of Birmingham steam locomotive was moved to the now-demolished Science Museum in 1966. It was taken there by road and lowered on to rails and the walls and roof of the museum were then built around it.

The Cube, so called because of its shape, had the honour of having the deepest hole in Birmingham during the construction phase. It was 20 metres deep and on looking into it, so to speak, it was discovered that 60,000 cubic metres of soil was excavated to leave a hole that was, apparently, large enough to hold 7,211 new Minis, although no one has thought to question the sanity of the person who came up with that statistic!

The Children's Hospital at Five Ways was built between 1913 and 1919 with the help of 450 children, presumably healthy ones, who were each given a souvenir trowel and laid their own individual bricks. This raised £24,000 for the building which was officially called the King Edward VII Memorial Hospital. The hospital has since moved to the site of the General Hospital and the Five Ways site is now an entertainment complex called Broadway Plaza.

In the First World War workers at the Austin car factory at Longbridge began making munitions rather than cars, and extra staff were taken on and accommodated in a new estate, which became known as Austin Village in Longbridge. The buildings were made up of timber bungalows shipped from USA. They came in kit form and were erected in one day. Each of the 300 or so homes had three bedrooms, a kitchen, bathroom and indoor toilet and was the brainchild of car industry supremo Herbert Austin.

A 200-year-old hovel in Erdington was sold recently for around £50,000. It is estimated that it would have sold for the equivalent of 2½p at the time it was built in around 1801. It was last lived in in 1992.

During European Architectural Year in 1975 Birmingham unveiled a kiosk on Edmund Street, which was to become a control point for the nearby underground car park. Gone was the familiar wooden hut on wheels, and in came a futuristic tinted glass tardis structure with built-in loo and central heating. It was immediately labelled 'the costliest sentry box in Britain' and is still there today.

A massive feature of the main city centre railway station at New Street was an iron and glass arched roof that was 1,100ft long, 205ft wide and 80ft high.

BT Tower was built of 6,000 tons of reinforced concrete. It was designed to handle 150,000 telephone calls simultaneously. It has been calculated that even in the strongest winds the top of the tower never moves more than 4½ inches.

Selly Manor, a timbered house, was due to be demolished in 1907 until nearby resident George Cadbury rescued it, taking it apart and moving into his estate and where it was rebuilt brick by brick.

Minworth Greaves House sits, today at least, near to Selly Manor, after being erected there after being moved brick by brick from its original location near Minworth. It was the idea of another member of the Cadbury family, Laurence, who bought it in 1911. It was reopened in 1932.

SHOPS & SHOPPING

Comedian Jasper Carrott once worked as a trainee buyer at a city centre department store called The Beehive with schoolfriend Bev Bevan of ELO fame.

TASCOS (The Ten Acres & Stirchley Co-op Society) was set up in 1875 in south-west Birmingham, then part of Worcestershire. It became part of the main Co-op in 1971.

It was announced in January 1991 that Lewis's department store was to close. In the Second World War it had a 'shadow hospital' with an x-ray machine and an operating theatre in the basement.

Bull Street was home to the department store Grey's, set up by Edward Greey, who dropped an e from his name to make it easier to recognise and easier for trading purposes. It was established in one small shop and expanded along the street knocking down dividing walls between them. Just after the Second World War it was taken over by Debenhams. It was closed in 1983 and demolished.

Barrows department store was the city's top grocery store for over 150 years, moving into Corporation Street in 1964, before closing at Christmas 1973.

The Fort Shopping Park opened in 1997 on a site that was formerly used as Dunlop's tyre-testing track. Among the shops was HMV's 100th store, a bit of a record that!

At the Fort development, construction teams had to remove 75,000 cubic metres of rubber, wood and masonry and infill the site with 94,000 cubic metres of rock sand and then used 300,000 masonry blocks, 30,000 cubic metres of concrete and a further 10,000 tonnes of precast concrete slabs.

Rackhams store on Corporation Street, now House of Fraser, was opened as a textile shop in 1851 by Wilkinson & Riddell. John

Rackham joined them around ten years later and eventually took control and expanded the premises. It has been part of the House of Fraser group since 1959 but it wasn't until 2003 that the name Rackhams was officially dropped, but locals still call it Rackhams, especially when referring to the back of it!

Woolworths opened in Birmingham in the Bullring 1921 and soon set up shops in the suburbs. The store remained in the Bullring until 1986. As the business folded the main city store was in the Pallasades shopping centre. At the height of their fame Woolies were opening one new store every eighteen days across the UK.

8

TRANSPORT

TRAMS

Hockley was the first place in Birmingham to be connected to the town centre by a tram line, opened in 1873.

Birmingham opened the first overhead electric line on the Bristol Road on 13 May 1901.

By June 1902 the City of Birmingham Tramways Company were operating 21 overhead electric trams, 54 cable trams, 89 steam engines, 76 double-decker steam trams, 10 horse cars and 45 horse buses.

Birmingham Corporation Tramways operated the largest narrow-gauge tramway network in the UK, built to a gauge of 3ft 6in. It was the fourth largest tramway network in the UK.

There were a total of 843 trams, with a maximum of 825 in service at any one time, 20 depots, 45 main routes and a total route length of 80½ miles.

On 4 July 1953, the last three routes to Short Heath, Pype Hayes and Erdington closed simultaneously and over seventy years of tramway operations in Birmingham came to an end.

The modern tram network known as the Metro got under way in November 1995 when the Transport Minister, Sir George Young, operated a mechanical digger to turn over the first sod of earth at the West Bromwich station.

The first Metro ran on a secret test run on 16 June 1998 and the line took its first paying passengers on 31 May 1999.

Line 1, as it is optimistically called, is 12½ miles in length and runs between Birmingham Snow Hill and Wolverhampton and runs mostly along the trackbed of the former Great Western Railway.

There are 23 stops on the Metro line.

The Hawthorns station is built on the site of the Hawthorns Halt railway station which was opened by the Great Western Railway on 31 December 1931, on their line from Birmingham Snow Hill to Wolverhampton Low Level. It mainly served football specials for nearby West Bromwich Albion. It was last used in April 1968.

Snow Hill railway station was reopened in 1987, a new building on the site of the former Great Western Railway station.

It was suggested that tram 13 which had been struck twice by lightning would be renamed '12a' to avoid future problems.

There are 16 low-floor trams in the fleet, two-car articulated vehicles built by Ansaldo of Italy.

Thirteen of the trams have been named as follows:

Ray Lewis: Director of Technical Services for Wolverhampton City Council during construction of the Midland Metro.

Frank Whittle: The Coventry-born inventor of the jet engine.

Sister Dora: A nineteenth-century nun and nurse in Walsall who was often likened to Florence Nightingale.

Alan Garner: Councillor for twenty years with transport interest.

John Stanley Webb: A Walsall-born journalist who wrote many national and internationally published books on tramways around the world, including *Tramways of the Black Country*.

Theresa Stewart: Former leader of Birmingham City Council.

Anthony Nolan: A charity is named after Anthony Nolan, who died in 1979 from a rare blood disorder.

James Eames: A former lord mayor and Birmingham Councillor, Honorary Alderman Eric James Eames.

Joseph Chamberlain: For twenty-five years he was a dominant figure in local politics. Domestic gas, electricity, the demolition of slums and the creation of Corporation Street were all his ideas.

Jeff Astle: Former West Brom and England centre-forward.

Billy Wright: The Wolves centre-half made 490 appearances for the Molineux side from 1939 to 1959 and gained 105 caps for England.

Agenoria: On 2 June 1829 large crowds saw the new-fangled engine called *Agenoria* haul eight carriages with 364 passengers and four carriages with 3½ tons of coal along the 2-mile level stretch of track. It is now in the National Railway Museum in York.

Gerwyn John: A former engineer who was systems operator for the Metro.

A CERTAIN TRAIN OF THOUGHT

The locomotive in the city's Millennium Point gallery, *The City of Birmingham,* made its last trip under steam on 19 May 1966 from Crewe to Lawley Street then by road to the old Science Museum. In her twenty-five years of service she travelled 1,650,000 miles, the equivalent of 66 times around the world.

The climb on the railway line between Cheltenham and Birmingham is so steep near Bromsgrove that the front of a train (depending on its length) can be 25ft higher than the back. In 1840 an experimental locomotive exploded when building up steam pressure, killing two crew members, Thomas Scaife and Joseph Rutherford, who are buried in Bromsgrove churchyard.

One of the largest bridges ever erected at the time was at Aston on 25 March 1906, when a 300-ton structure was placed in position in just 15½ minutes. Today it would take longer just to layout the traffic cones and distribute the health and safety briefing!

When Snow Hill station opened in October 1852 a special eve-of-opening train *Lord of the Isles* was derailed on route and arrived the next day after a change of engine.

After 26 years, on Friday 27 September 2002, Les Ross presented his final BRMB Radio show live from Birmingham International station where a train was named *Les Ross* by Virgin Trains. He has since preserved this locomotive following its retirement from passenger service.

New Street station was erected on a run-down slum area of the town centre known as The Froggery. The site was said to have cost £500,000 to clear and that was over 150 years ago. Three chapels, a burial ground, a synagogue and a theatre were among the buildings demolished. The first train left the station on 1 June 1854.

At the time of completion, New Street station had the largest iron and glass roof in the world. It was removed in the name of progress during redevelopment of 1967.

Currently over 140,000 passengers use New Street satation every day, more than double the number it was designed to handle. A major redevlopment project is underway that will create a new concourse with three and half times more space for passengers than currently exists. It is scheduled to open in 2015.

THE INNER RING ROAD

The Minister of Transport and Aviation, Harold Watkinson, officially inaugurated the Inner Ring Road scheme on 8 March 1957 and it opened three years later.

The scheme consisted of 3¾ miles of dual carriageway.

The scheme involved the acquisition of 1,500 properties over 80 acres of land.

The complete circuit of the Ring Road was first used on 4 January 1971 and officially opened by the queen on 7 April 1971.

FACTS TO UNTANGLE ABOUT SPAGHETTI JUNCTION

Spaghetti Junction is the nickname of one of the most complicated-looking motorway junctions in Europe. It is officially known as the Midland Link Gravelly Hill Interchange.

It was nicknamed Spaghetti Junction by *Birmingham Evening Mail* journalist Roy Smith because of its distinctive shape, and not because it is 'pasta' joke to drive on or because they made a right 'Bolognese' of the whole thing.

Motorists reach the junction from Birmingham via a link road, the A38M, better known as the Aston Expressway. This was the most expensive stretch of road at the time costing £7 million per mile. The cost was partially explained by the fact it was one of the first routes to go through an urban area rather through cheaper countryside. It eventually cost around £24 million in total.

One of the early proposals was to have roadways painted in distinctive colours such as yellow; red and green so drivers could follow coded routes.

1,500 people were rehoused and around 160 houses and a block of flats were demolished to make way for it.

A bank, a pub and an inconveniently located public convenience were also demolished.

Work started in 1968 and it was completed in 1972.

In the first twenty years it was estimated that 700 million vehicles had travelled through the junction.

40,000 vehicles a day used it when it first opened, and it was expected that the numbers of vehicles would eventually double to 80,000. Today that figure has again been doubled to around 160,000.

It is elevated for 3½ miles.

It contains 1,200 crossbeams and 3,600 columns.

175,000 cubic yards of concrete were poured into it.

There are 30 acres of tarmac.

Salford Pool beneath it was reduced in size from 15.5 to 11 acres.

The junction was given the go-ahead by Transport Secretary Barbara Castle on 20 January 1967 and was opened by Transport Minister Peter Walker on 24 May 1972.

The first private vehicle through the complex carried a bouquet of 243 red roses, a gift from the Lord Mayor of London, symbolising the distance in miles between London and Lancaster, where the M6 ended.

ANY ROAD UP

Birmingham's first traffic island opened at Six Ways, Erdington, in 1926. It was also the first traffic island outside London.

The traffic island on the A41 leading from Birmingham to West Bromwich at the M5 junction was built around the remains of the eighteenth-century Sandwell Lodge, the remaining arch is suffering under the vibration of pounding traffic.

Worker Lewis Skinner removed the last old-style parking meter nearly 28 years after he installed the first ones in April 1963.

The first driver on the M1 when it opened in 1959 was known as Dick Turpin; Edwin Turpin was heading for Birmingham from Northampton when he passed the junction at just the right time. Not only did he get home earlier than he would have hoped but he had the honour of appearing in the *Northampton Chronicle & Echo*.

A bridge over the A38 at Longbridge was not used by pedestrians but by cars, 360,000 per year to be precise, but none of the vehicles had ever been seen in public at the time because it was built to carry the production line from the west works to the south works of the Austin/Rover car factory in 1971. It was the longest production line in Europe. The famous conveyor bridge was dismantled during the demolition of the factory in August 2006, with the help of a 1,000-tonne crane. The main section of the bridge was 510ft long and weighed 500 tonnes. The Austin Allegro model was the first type of vehicle to use the twin-track bridge.

In August 2010 the road bridge over the railway near St Andrew's football ground was replaced to enable larger trains to pass beneath it, allowing continental-style freight trains to reach the north from the continent, taking 50,000 lorries off the M6 – or at least that was the theory! The bridge carried not only thousands of football fans but also cables and pipes and twenty BT telephone lines, eight Virgin lines and a sewer pipe had to be moved at a cost of £2 million. Who would have thought replacing a bridge could be so complicated?

Some of the oldest bridges in Birmingham are to be found on the canals, or more specifically across the canals. Those around the Brindleyplace area, for instance, date from 1827 and were made of iron in Black Country factories and, conveniently, shipped by canal.

The Birmingham stagecoach left from the Swan, on the site of the Bullring, on 24 May 1731. It took two-and-a-half days to reach London via Warwick.

The Watch Committee set up the first purpose-built horse-drawn ambulance in 1901 after a serious fire resulted in injured men being taken to hospital on handcarts. Today there is a fleet of 350 ambulances in 25 stations across the West Midlands.

A group called the 'Road Safety Analysis' released the results of a survey in August 2010 that showed that 1 child in 332 was at risk of bring hurt in a road traffic accident, making Birmingham the fifty-eighth worst place to be injured.

Of all the journeys made in Birmingham, 42 per cent are under 2km. This is a distance that a person of average fitness can readily walk in 20–25 minutes.

A new aqueduct opened at Selly Oak in February 2011. The £1.6 million structure is the largest aqueduct built on site in Europe.

FOR WHOM THE ROAD TOLLS

The M6 toll road cost £900 million to build, over £1 billion if you include the design and planning costs.

The 27-mile route was billed as the solution to congestion on the busiest stretch of motorway in Europe – that's the M6 north of the city.

Site clearance began in November 2000 and construction in April 2001. It opened on 9 December 2003.

9,613 tonnes of structural steel were used in its construction, that's the same amount used on the Eiffel Tower.

After people got used to it, 60,000 vehicles travelled along it each day, but since that peak in Spring 2006 around 40,000–45,000 vehicles use it.

The five millionth vehicle used it on 29 April 2004.

MOTORWAY LIST OF SHAME

A November 2010 survey by the traffic information company INREX revealed Birmingham has the worst traffic jams in the country. The section of the M5 near the M6 junction was found to be jammed 63 hours a week in 2009/10 with an average speed below 15mph when congested. I'm not sure how they could tell, but Wednesday is apparently the worst day for traffic jams!

The top ten most congested areas in the Birmingham area are:

M6 J8 North
M6 link Birmingham
End of link to M5 South
J8 North M5 link
J8 South M5 link
J10 Wolverhampton East
J9 Wednesbury for Birmingham
J9 Wednesbury for Stoke-on-Trent
J1 West Bromwich
J7 Birmingham North

MOVE ALONG THE BUS PLEASE

The first horse-drawn bus service began on 5 May 1834 with horses trotting from Snow Hill to the Bristol Road and back. If you wanted to go anywhere else you'd have to have waited two months, because that's when the next route began operating. And you thought you waited ages for a bus today!

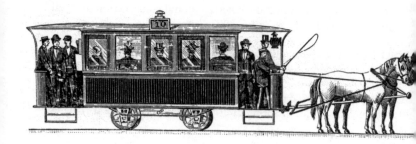

The route from Ladywood to the city centre via Icknield Port Road and Holloway Head was tram route 33, this became bus route 95, which became the 43, then the 66 and is now the 80, but the 66 still exists and goes elsewhere!

Birmingham's most famous bus route is the Outer Circle no. 11 which travels around the outer ring of the city, hence the title. It is the longest urban bus route in Europe, carrying over 18 million passengers every year. It takes over two hours to go full-circle, unless you're in a rush in which case it will stop at all 266 stops and take three hours!

At busy periods, forty-two buses work the Outer Circle timetable, clocking up a combined 15 million miles every year. The route serves twenty-five major bus, rail or Metro interchanges, nineteen shopping centres, six hospitals and over forty public houses.

The no. 8 Inner Circle route was featured in a brilliant play, *Go and Play Up Your Own End* by Brummie playwright and comedian Malcolm Stent in 1998.

To commemorate fifty years of bus services on Bristol Road and in recognition of the queen's Golden Jubilee, Travel West Midlands rebranded the 61, 62 and 63 routes the Jubilee Line and introduced thirty-six easy access buses in September 2002.

In 2011 National Express West Midlands, the major operator of bus routes across the city, produced posters stating: 'the moon is 238,897 miles away. We take you there 290 times every year'. Most people would prefer to be able to get a no. 11 without having to wait for the bus to get back from the moon!

Centro says there are now over 6,400 free Park and Ride car parking spaces in the West Midlands as a whole. These spaces are calculated to take over 53,000 journeys off the road per week, saving 66,000 litres of fuel. This is the equivalent to 94 tankers a year.

UP, UP AND AWAY!

During Birmingham's first flying demonstration, in 1911, Bentfield C. Hucks flew a Blériot monoplane from Castle Bromwich airfield.

On 9 July 1939 the Duchess of Kent officially opened Birmingham's Elmdon airport. The weather was so bad she couldn't fly back to London.

The first passenger jumbo jet arrived at Birmingham Airport on 12 March 1979. Aer Lingus operated it for the Cheltenham horse racing festival, bringing punters across the Irish Sea for the famous event.

9

EDUCATION MATTERS

EARLY EDUCATION

George Dixon, MP for Birmingham, and Joseph Chamberlain, Mayor of Birmingham, both nonconformists, were leaders of the National Education League and campaigners in the 1860s and 1870s for the provision of education free of influence by the churches.

After the Forster Elementary Education Act 1870 Birmingham set up council-run schools, or Board schools.

THE FIVE BOARD SCHOOLS
OPENED IN 1873

Bloomsbury, Dartmouth Street, opened in March 1873
Jenkins Street, May 1873
Farm Street, July 1873
Steward Street, July 1873
Garrison Lane, July 1873

Today there are around 430 schools in the city.

Education in Birmingham is delivered according to five key outcomes
identified in the Children Act 2004:

Be healthy   Stay safe
Enjoy and achieve   Make a positive contribution
Achieve economic well-being

DIDN'T YOU USED TO GO TO . . . ?

Birmingham schools have produced an eclectic mix of students who
have gone on to successful careers in a wide variety of occupations,
for instance:

Jasper Carrott was educated at Acocks Green Infants & Junior School
and Moseley Grammar School.

TV wrestler Steve Logan attended Primrose Hill Comprehensive
School in Kings Norton.

DJ and TV presenter Catherine 'Cat' Deeley, born in October 1976,
attended Grove Vale Infant School in Great Barr and Sutton Coldfield
Grammar School for Girls.

Charles Douglas Flello, born in January 1966, is Labour MP for
Stoke-on-Trent South and both he and Enoch Powell attended Kings
Norton Boys' School.

Clewley Freeman played professional football for England scoring
three goals in five appearances, and won the FA Cup with Burnley in
1914. He was born in Handsworth and attended Gower Street School
in Aston.

Ian Lavender, actor, who played the 'stupid boy' Private Pike, in the long-running BBC comedy series *Dad's Army*, attended Bournville Grammar Technical School for Boys.

Lee Carsley the former Birmingham City and Republic of Ireland midfielder and Craig Gardner, Sunderland midfielder who was in Birmingham City's Carling Cup-winning side in 2011, both attended Cockshut Hill School in Yardley.

Andy Akinwolere, presenter of Blue Peter, former footballer Darren Bradley and Ian Ashbee of Preston North End all attended St Thomas Aquinas Catholic School in Kings Norton.

The 1960s chart-topping band The Rockin' Berries first formed while several members were pupils at Turves Green Boys' School.

Anthony Carthew, ITN News reporter; Bev Bevan, musician; Carl Chinn, historian and broadcaster; and Gladstone Small, cricketer, are all former pupils of Moseley Grammar School/Moseley School.

Gabriel Agbonlahor of Aston Villa and Michael Ricketts, once of Bolton Wanderers, both attended St Edmund Campion Catholic School in Erdington.

Ian Taylor and Lee Hendrie, both former Aston Villa players, attended Washwood Heath School.

Sir Michael Checkland, Director General of the BBC from 1987 to 1992 and Oscar Deutsch (1893–1941), the founder of the Odeon Cinema chain in the United Kingdom are two ex-pupils of King Edward's School, Five Ways.

THE EIGHT NOBEL PRIZE WINNERS WHO ATTENDED BIRMINGHAM UNIVERSITY

Lord Robert Cecil received the Nobel Peace Prize in 1937 for his services to the League of Nations while chancellor at Birmingham University.

Sir Paul Nurse, biochemist, won the 2001 Nobel Prize in Physiology and Medicine for his work on cells.

Maurice Wilkins received the Nobel Prize in 1962 for his work in the discovery of the structure of DNA and its importance in transferring information in living material. At the age of six, Wilkins was brought to England from his native New Zealand and educated at King Edward's School, Birmingham.

Francis Aston was presented with the Nobel Prize for Chemistry in 1922. He invented the mass spectroscope to separate isotopes of neon by taking advantage of their slight differences in mass. He grew up in Tennal House, Harborne, and a blue plaque was erected in 2007 on a house near to where the house stood.

Sir Norman Haworth won the Nobel Prize for Chemistry 1937 'for his investigations on carbohydrates and vitamin C'.

Sir John R. Vane was a pharmacologist whose work with aspirin and the prostaglandin group of biochemical compounds earned him a Nobel Prize for Medicine in 1982.

Professor Peter Bullock worked on sustainable resources and climate change and was awarded the Nobel Peace Prize in 2007.

Sir Peter Medawar received the Nobel Prize in Physiology and Medicine 1960 for discovering acquired immunological tolerance.

INVENTIONS & INVENTORS – PATENTLY A GOOD IDEA

George Muntz was a Birmingham MP between 1840 and 1857 and was big in copper in the nineteenth century. He took out a metal patent devising a combination of 60 per cent copper and 40 per cent zinc, which was used for ships' hulls and corroded at a slower rate than normal metal. This made him his fortune.

In 1878 Joseph Hudson made the first whistle ever to be used by a football referee. It was used for the first time at a game held at Nottingham Forest. Prior to this referees used handkerchiefs to attract players' attention. Hudson also invented the 'Acme Thunderer', the first ever pea whistle, that remains the most used whistle in the world.

On 7 April 1902 the Teasmade was patented by gunsmith Frank Clarke. It was sold as 'A Clock That Makes Tea!', however, the original machine and all rights to it were said to have been purchased from Albert Richardson. Frank Clarke later made several important patents to the air pistol.

A manually-powered domestic vacuum cleaner was invented, in 1905, by manufacturer Walter Griffiths of Conybere Street, Highgate. It was originally patented as 'Griffiths' Improved Vacuum Apparatus for Removing Dust from Carpets'.

In 1921 a British patent for windscreen wipers was registered by Mills Munitions, the same company which manufactured hand grenades, or Mills Bombs.

On 7 May 1802, Edward Thomason was granted a patent for the design of the modern corkscrew. Thomason, the son of a Birmingham bucklemaker, invented it in 1796 and his factory in Church Street went to make 130,000 of them. Each corkscrew carried the motto, 'Ne Plus Ultra' which means 'None Better' and you'd have to be bitter and twisted not to agree.

In 1840 Henry Holland was the first to patent ribs of tubular steel with fittings for an umbrella. Previously whale bone or cane had been used.

YET MORE INVENTIVE BRUMMIE-RELATED THINGS . . .

George Elkington, who lived in St Paul's Square, pioneered electroplating for metal products using potassium cyanide. His factory became the Science Museum.

Alexander Parkes, a worker at Elkington's, invented the first plastic which at the time he called Parkesine, and the process was later refined to produce celluloid.

Conway Berners-Lee is a mathematician and computer scientist who worked in the team that developed the Ferranti Mark 1, the world's first commercial stored programmed electronic computer. He was born in Birmingham in 1921 and is the father of Sir Tim Berners-Lee, the inventor of the internet.

In 1880 Gamgee Tissue was invented by Joseph Sampson Gamgee, a surgical dressing which has a thick layer of absorbent cotton wool between two layers of absorbent gauze. It represents the first use of cotton wool in a medical context, and was a major advancement in the prevention of infection of surgical wounds. It is still the basis for many modern surgical dressings.

James Watt of steam engine fame invented the first copier in 1778 at his Soho Works in Handsworth. It worked by pressing a document written in ink against a sheet of damp semi-transparent paper.

The Birmingham firm of Evans Electronic Developments invented a heater which was installed beneath typewriter keyboards and emitted enough heat to make typing in cold climates comfortable 'without injury to the paintwork of the machine'.

WE DON'T NEED NO EDUCASHUN – EXTRACTS FROM SCHOOL LOG BOOKS

29 January 1892
'Called attention to the bad lighting of the middle of the school and recommended that the ceiling be painted white.'

29 January 1904
'Dr Caroline O'Carroll visited to examine boys of weak or defective intellect with a view to their admission to the Special Classes.'

29 January 1915
'The Canadian Government sent gifts of salmon. Eighteen tins were allocated to this school and the poorest children were given a tin today.'

9 February 1876
'So many boys come late in the afternoon, never less than 20 or 30, and sometimes, as this afternoon, about 60. Each latecomer has the cane once on one hand, with the exception of those bringing a note with a reasonable excuse.'

17 February 1909
'Roasting lesson, meat & gravy satisfactory, cabbage boiled very carefully.'

4 March 1948
'F.S. was taken home by Miss Phelps as he had put a piece of chalk up his nose and could not get it down. His mother took him to the doctors who removed the chalk, and he returned to school.'

11 March 1937
'Closed today due to inclement weather. Boots and clothing of the 21 children who arrived were in such a condition that it would have been injurious to children's health if they were allowed to remain at school.'

18 March 1920
'There was a heavy fall of snow on Monday; consequently, the attendance on that day was very bad. The very poorest children came to school while the better class ones remained at home.'

22 March 1991
'At the last minute and because of severe weather conditions our Lenten School Mass was transferred from the Oratory to the school hall. Ironically our Lenten Appeal is in aid of the drought-stricken region of East Africa, a lack of water was not something our region suffered from this day.'

28 March 1890
'An attempt was made to prevent the boys coming to school. The instigators seemed chiefly boys who had left school and street ruffians. I went out and thumped two or three who began stone-throwing and the police came down at the time they went away.'

1 April 1968
'Six rabbits were born today at school and seven Mongolian gerbils.'

1 May 1946
'The telephone was installed in this Dept. No Edgbaston 3765, and has been fitted in the Head Teacher's room.'

3 May 1879
'Introduced a new system of desk drill. The class movements are to be done by marching in step.'

5 May 1907
'Test results in each standard are very satisfactory, although there is a dull batch of boys in Standard V.'

6 May 1926
'Mr — has applied for a transfer "to a school in the suburbs in consequence of eye trouble resulting from the smoky area and the constant use of electric light in the classroom." I have acceded to his request.'

15 May 1906
'Mr Atkinson's class commenced the drawing lesson with only half the pencils sharp. Mr A took until 2.35pm to prepare the remainder.'

22 May 1969
'Whilst making a run for the rabbits and guinea pigs from an old bookcase it fell upon the head teacher's foot damaging the big toe.'

23 May 1978
'The caretaker's kitten stuck its head in an electric kettle and had to be taken to the fire station to be released.'

29 May 1929
'On complaint of the Girls' School, the Boys' School also suffering, I went to see Bowkett Bros Clement Street, about a badly smoking chimney, giving out dense and acrid fumes. This has been a frequent source of trouble to the schools, and they promised to get the fires lighted earlier so that the worst of the troubles would be over before school began.'

30 May 1941
'The children collected £1 18s for cigarettes for the fighting forces.'

6 June 1901
'The caretaker has neglected to fill the school inkwells. As all the classes write on paper, work has been greatly hindered.'

25 June 1884

'The boy W — elder, a most disreputable boy, actually refused to do what he was told, point blank. Punishment was attempted to be inflicted, but the effect was a dreadful howl and kicking, before a stroke could be inflicted. His parents are I am afraid equally bad. I sent for the mother, but could not make her see his error. The case is one for expulsion. He is altogether so much worse, morally, than the other boys that he ought to be expelled.'

3 July 1884

'Because of the bad state of the walls of the gardens in Beaufort Road, and Plough and Harrow Road, covered with chalk marks, writing, etc done by children in these schools, I have put two boys on two afternoons of this week to scrub them.'

9 July 1897

'Holiday given on 7th for Royal Visit on the opening of the new General Hospital. Attendance poor on the following morning.'

20 July 1945

'On Wednesday a child in Jr IV was bundled out of the room for bad behaviour. Five minutes later her mother came to school and went straight to the teacher in question. She used foul and abusive language and threatened to do her bodily injury . . . by brandishing a milk bottle. I reported the case immediately to the office and wrote to the mother asking for an apology. The case is proceeding but no apology up to now is forthcoming.'

6 September 1905

'It was necessary to tell Mr P— that he must not box boys on the ears.'

11 September 1941

'Twelve children were excluded as being verminous. This is the result of so many mothers being engaged in war work.'

19 September 1873

'At the ordinary singing lesson this afternoon I taught the Fire Brigade.'

19 September 1966

'Television programmes for schools commenced today. We have inherited the Secondary Boys' television set at a yearly rental of £40 plus £5 licence.'

23 September 1931
'The school dental surgeon carried out an inspection of the 248 boys then present. The examination showed that 231 boys need treatment.'

30 September 1938
'This has been a nerve racking week for we have been on the verge of a great European war. Instructions have been arriving for fitting gas masks; evacuating children into the country; and holding of parents' meetings rearrangements for the evacuation. Into the bargain the weather has been at its worst – real black days [with] torrential rain. When things were at the blackest an arrangement was made that the Prime Minister, Mr Neville Camberlain, was once again flying to Germany for a personal interview with Herr Hitler. Then there was further suspense – then great relief – Peace act signed – Peace in Europe in our day.'

3 October 1902
'On Wednesday afternoon the round window at the end of the schoolroom fell in, fortunately hurting no one. Teachers and children have suffered very much from the keenness of the wind blowing through the open space and may have very bad colds.'

12 October 1928
'On Tuesday last, the children had a Schubert Centenary Concert. Messrs Dale Forty & Co. kindly lent a Columbian gramophone and Schubert records.'

13 October 1967
'44 dual tables with Formica tops delivered. Three classrooms now have Formica topped tables.'

15 October 1974
'The gas was out from 2.00pm to allow gas engineers to check for North Sea gas fitting.'

17 October 1930
'Some of the children have very bad boots at the present time and there is little prospect of some of them getting new boots as a large percentage of the parents are unemployed.'

18 October 1940
'On the night of the 15th Birmingham experienced its most terrifying night. From 8pm till 4am bombs dropped incessantly. Next day hardly any children arrived in school. The next two nights were just as bad so nerves and work have been at a low standard this week.'

21 October 1910
'Two children who were verminous, were taken to the city cleaning station to be cleansed by order of the Medical Officer of Health.'

4 November 1891
'Punished Smith of Standard V for wilfully breaking a school slate by jumping upon it.'

28 October 1966
'£10 sent to Aberfan Disaster Fund.'

29 October 1937
'The "Audiometer" test took place last Monday morning. There wee 88 children tested – ages between 11 and 14. Of these some 18 children were found to be deaf. For the time being, these children have been placed in front desks in class. A further test will be taken later on.'

31 October 1882
'Very grieved to say that a 1st Class lad was found passing papers to other lads in the class on which he had written the foulest and filthiest language. I sent him home and have put the matter in the hands of the Rev.' (The following week the lad was 'dismissed from the school'.)

8 November 1912
'On Wednesday morning some thirty of the first class children paid a visit to the Chrysanthemum show.'

1 December 1914
'The Lady Mayoress Mrs Bowater, visited us on Thursday morning to thank the children for the pillows they had made for our soldiers.'

3 December 1900
'Attendance very poor about 50 children being absent on account of measles.'

6 December 1926
'Examinations in full swing, it is surprising to find a high proportion of marks in arithmetic thrown away through trivial mistakes.'

8 December 1982
'Nursery visited the City to pay a visit to Father Christmas at Rackhams but a power cut sent them to Lewis's instead.'

10

THE INDUSTRIAL SCENE

WORKSHOP OF THE WORLD

Birmingham used to be known as 'The City of a Thousand Trades'.

The first canal boat bringing coal to Birmingham from the Black Country arrived on 6 November 1769. A huge canal network was subsequently established and even today Birmingham has 22 more miles of canals than Venice.

Charles Henry Foyle was the inventor of the folding carton and founder of Boxfoldia Company. He set up a trust 1940 with an endowment of shares in his company. The trust supported education and educational activities for children. Charles was related to Christina Foyle, the owner of Foyles bookshop

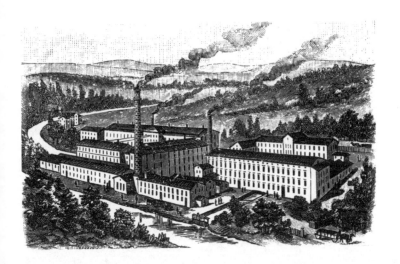

The Chad Valley Toy Company takes its name from the small river in Harborne near to the factory. They first produced soft toys including a range of fourteen different sizes of teddy bears. Chad Valley was taken over by Palitoy in 1978 and Woolworths acquired the trade name in 1988.

Joseph Gillott was a well-known pen maker who claimed, on his wedding day, to have produced a gross of pens and sold them to the congregation for a shilling each. When 'his nibs' died in 1872, he left an estate worth £250,000, around £17 million in today's money.

Wing Yip and family were thought to be worth £30 million in 1996. Wing Yip came from China via Hong Kong in the late 1950s and from 1970 built up the Oriental foods business for which he is well known.

The council compulsorily purchased private water businesses in 1875 to set up the water department. At that time Birmingham used around 20 million gallons of water per day. Today Birmingham swallows up over 60 million gallons per day. Birmingham set about getting more water to supply its thirsty industry and population; a 70-mile aqueduct was built between the Elan Valley in Mid-Wales and Bartley Green in Birmingham.

The huge former factory that dominates the skyline off the M6 near Spaghetti Junction is known as Fort Dunlop, the former Dunlop tyre manufactory, but why the word Fort is used is not known. There are, however, a couple of theories; firstly, when it was built in 1916, it was on a green field site and stood out like a castle or fort. The other theory that I never 'tyre' of repeating, is that workers arriving there via barge from the city centre were greeted by the bargees shouting 'For Dunlop'.

The Midland Vinegar Company commenced production in 1875 and twenty-five years later started producing HP sauce. No one can say for sure, but it seems likely that the HP initials were a marketing ploy, with the Houses of Parliament printed on the bottles indicating it was well regarded, although many MPs may have thought they had a sauce for using their building to advertise it. In 1883 two workers drowned in a vat of vinegar.

TEN BUSINESSES FROM 1940
WHICH WERE IN DECLINE

The Empire Folding Car Co., Summer Row, perambulator manufacturer.

Davis & Wilson, Conybere Street, chimney sweeping machine manufacturer, Eiffel Tower brand.

Edgbaston Firelighters & Chemicals Ltd, Belgrave Road, stick firelighters and bundled firewood.

Clear Hooters Ltd, Hampton Street, horn manufacturer.

The Gray Horse Shoe Pad Co. Ltd, Suffolk Street, horse clothing manufacturer.

Sodazone Ltd, Hurst Street, soda fountain manufacturer.

Prestox Co., Cannon Street, insecticide manufacturer (for beetles, cockroaches, ants, etc.).

The Italian Trading Co. Ltd, Frederick Street, pearl stringers.

Charles Adderley, Berners Street, sawdust dealers.

Wolseley Sheep Shearing Machine Co. Ltd, electric sheep-clippers.

SIX TRADE ASSOCIATIONS FROM 1937

Birmingham and District Butchers' and Pork Butchers' Trade and Benevolent Association

Birmingham and District Mineral Water Manufacturers and Bottlers' Association Limited

Birmingham Fish, Game and Poultry Dealers' Association

Black Bolt and Nut Manufacturers' Association of Great Britain

Galvanised Tank Manufacturers' Association

National Leather Goods and Saddlery Manufacturers' Association

MAKING A MINT, TO COIN A PHRASE

The Birmingham Mint, under the direction of the Heaton family, manufactured coins and coin blanks for countries all over the world.

Most, if not all, of the copper coinage of pence, half pence and farthings at the Royal Mint in London were produced on Heaton's blanks in 1851.

10 million blanks for 1 cent Canadian coins were shipped in 1858.

Heaton provided the blanks for all of Norway and Sweden's production of one, two and five øre coins from at least 1876 to 1920.

4 million copper nickel 2½ centavos were struck for Columbia in 1881.

In 1892 over 37 million bronze and silver blanks were shipped to Portugal.

35 tons of blanks for the Indian market were lost at sea in 1857.

In 1893 about 100 tons of copper blanks were sent to Bushire, Persia, finally arriving by mules on a 1,000-mile overland journey.

In 1904 China obtained 117 million bronze blanks, amounting to 880 tons.

Most of Iran's copper nickel 5 rials were struck in the Tehran Mint on blanks from Brum in 1965.

Over 3 million 2 centésimos were produced for Uruguay in 1954.

In 1957 newly independent Ghana received 15 million 2s coins.

In 1967, 27 million blanks were sent to Singapore for 1 and 5 cent coins.

The mint's first business in Eire was struck in 1968 when 25 million coins were struck.

31 million blanks, or planchets, were provided in 1970 for Vienna's 5 schilling pieces.

When Britain changed to decimal currency the Royal Mint in London was provided with 1,680 tons of new penny bronze blanks and 466 tons of ten new pence copper nickel blanks.

THEY DON'T MAKE THEM LIKE THAT ANYMORE – VICTORIAN INDUSTRIES THAT SEEM TO HAVE DISAPPEARED

Thomas Hurst, artificial eye manufacturers

Frederick Green, bone boilers

F. & C. Osler, chandelier manufacturers

William Evans, dog muzzle makers

Barnard & Co., egg boilermakers

Charles Bassett, fender makers

P. Wilson, gunpowder manufacturers

William Sames, harmonium manufacturers

Geo. Chambers, ivory, bone and wood turner

Troman Bros, Jew's harp makers

Joseph Titcombe, knitting pin manufacturer

Robert Mole & Sons, lance and javelin manufacturer

Eastgate & Sons, magic-lantern makers

J. Gilbert, nutcracker manufacturers

A. Archer, oil-can makers

James Collins, pulley makers

Wynn & Co., quoit makers

Steven Armstrong, rivet makers

Berkeley & Co., sardine tin opener makers

Henry Tibbins, toasting fork manufacturers (telescopic)

Brindley & Gell, umbrella and parasol manufacturers (rib and stretch)

William Canning, varnish manufacturers

Arthur Dales, watercress dealers

Fred Bubb, yeast importers

Edmund Boughton, zinc merchants

CHOCK-A-BLOCK WITH FACTS ABOUT CADBURY'S

John Cadbury opened a shop at 93 Bull Street in 1824 selling tea, coffee and cocoa nibs. At that time the town had 100,000 inhabitants.

His business grew as the town expanded. In 1847 they moved to a factory on Bridge Street (where the Hyatt Hotel now stands), but later they sought a larger site away from the growing industrial areas.

The site was at Bournville, 4 miles from the town centre but on a canal and railway and with plenty of land for expansion and they moved there in 1879.

In 1879 they employed 230 workers and expanded to employ 5,000 workers by 1909.

Initially two-thirds of the workforce were women but none were married. It was thought married women would often stay at home to look after their children.

The company built a village for the workers, originally with around 300 homes.

The name Bournville came from the Bourn Brook and Cadbury added the French-sounding Ville to make the name more distictive. It was said good chocolates were made in France at the time and Cadbury liked the Gallic allusion as he thought it would be good for business.

Bournville Rest House was built to celebrate the Silver Wedding Anniversary of George and Elizabeth Cadbury, and was paid for by the employees of Cadbury Brothers Ltd.

By 1904 the death rate at Bournville was 6.9 per 1,000, compared with 19 per 1,000 in the city as a whole.

Today there are nearly 8,000 homes with 24,000 residents on what is known as the Bournville Village Trust, but today only around 40 per cent of people who live on the estates have a connection with Cadbury's.

CADBURY'S DAIRY MILK

Cadbury's most famous brand, Dairy Milk, went on sale in June 1904 with a 'far higher milk content than previously known'.

Cadbury considered three other names for the bar – Jersey, Highland Milk and Dairy Maid – before settling on Dairy Milk.

65 per cent of the population of Great Britain is said to have bought at least one Dairy Milk in a year.

Around 500 million bars are made in the UK each year at Bournville.

Since 1928 the brand has been advertised as 'a glass and a half of milk in every half pound bar of chocolate'.

Enough Dairy Milks are sold every year to cover every Premiership and npower Football League pitch, five times over.

The amount of milk used in a year's production of Dairy Milk chocolate would fill fourteen Olympic-size swimming pools.

CREME EGGS

Creme Eggs have been manufactured at Bournville since 1971.

200 million eggs are sold per year.

Cadbury's research shows that 53 per cent of people will bite off the top, lick out the goo and then eat the chocolate; 20 per cent of people will just bite straight through and 16 per cent of people use their finger to scoop out the creme.

If you piled all the Creme Eggs made in a year on top of each other, it would be ten times higher than Mount Everest.

ROSES: THEY GROW ON YOU!

Roses were first produced at Bournville in 1938.

If you stretched all the Roses chocolates sold in a year end to end, the line would stretch round the British coastline over three times.

Roses outsell frozen turkeys by 50 per cent during the Christmas period.

The most popular Rose is Hazelnut in Caramel.

80 per cent of Roses sales take place at Christmas and Easter.

Over 1.3 million boxes of Roses chocolates are sold every year in the UK, which is enough for 25 per person.

The original flavours of Roses were: plain chocolate, strawberry, coffee, fudge, gooseberry truffle, almond whirl, caramel, marzipan, turkish delight, almonds and dates.

The ten current varieties are: Brazilian Darkness, Dairy Milk, Golden Barrel, Caramel, Caramel Velvet, Country Fudge, Hazelnut in Caramel, Hazelnut Whirl, Strawberry Dream and Tangy Orange.

Norman Vaughan advertised Roses in the 1960s giving a thumbs-up while reciting the catchphrase: 'Swinging! Roses Grow On You'.

MORE CHOCOLATE BITES

Milk Tray was introduced in 1915, the name 'Tray' derived from the way in which they were delivered to the shops. Cadbury made nineteen TV adverts with a man delivering boxes to various ladies with the strap line, 'All because the lady loves Milk Tray'.

£38 million worth of Crunchie bars are sold in the UK each year.

The British consume around 80 million shell-type Easter Eggs each year, around 50 per cent of them will be Cadbury eggs.

Cadbury made its first creme-filled egg in 1923 and its first shell Easter Egg in 1875.

TEN GREAT SOUNDING VICTORIAN COMPANIES

North of England Preserves & Marmalade Company
Albion Mills Harness Manufacturing Company
The Midland Counties Aerated Bread Company
The India Rubber & Telegraph Works Co. Ltd
The Birmingham Pig & Cattle Sales Co. Ltd
The Patent Automatic Heat Regulator & Fire Alarm Company
Patent Weldless Steelchain & Cable Co. Ltd
Patent Oil Bath Axle Box & Fitting Company
South Staffordshire & Birmingham District Steam Tramway Co. Ltd
The Patent Metallic Airtight Coffin Company.

FACTS ABOUT THE JEWELLERY QUARTER: EVERY ONE'S A GEM

The oldest stone in the Jewellery Quarter is the Warstone, a boulder dumped there by a passing glacier from Scandinavia, too large for your finger but great for geologists.

The Argent Centre, originally the Albert Works, once contained a Turkish bath. A gold pen manufacturer recycled the steam.

Regent Row off Vittoria Street was once nicknamed Gooseberry Alley from a garden of gooseberry bushes that grew there.

The Birmingham Assay office is the largest in the world and has been operating since 1773.

The whistles used on the *Titanic* by the White Star Line were supplied in 1912 by J. Hudson & Co.

St Paul's Church is known as the Jewellers' Church and is in the centre of the city's last remaining Georgian square.

The Big Peg is a flattened factory, a 1971 building containing numerous small workshops. It is described on one website as, 'large rectangular sugar cube that crashed to the ground as a meteorite in the 1960s.'

The Chamberlain Clock is the centrepiece of the Jewellery Quarter. It survived two world wars but shortly before restoration in 1989 it was hit and damaged by a lorry!

A prominent structure is the Temple of Relief. It is an outdoor urinal erected in 1883.

Students of the School of Jewellery created gifts that could be presented to world leaders at the G8 Summit, in May 1998. Cherie Blair selected the winning entry.

Anongkarat Unyawong designed the 1998 Eurovision Song contest trophy in the School of Jewellery. It featured 25 swirling silver spines and one gold spine.

Prince Charles' gates were completed in 1991 in a building converted by the Duchy of Cornwall.

THE JEWELLERY QUARTER
FINDINGS TRAIL

There are 26 pavement plaques, which take you from Newhall Street in the city centre to the heart of the Jewellery Quarter and back. Each represents something related to activities in the area.

Going from Newhall Street to the Jewellery Quarter you walk past:

A) A tunnel sign which is above the entrace to 6 miles of communication tunnels beneath the city.

B) Precious metals symbol used in hallmarking.

C) Beer Bottle Tops, the anchor symbol of Birmingham's hallmarks which came from a pub, the Crown & Anchor, in London.

D) Church symbol represents St Paul's Church, in the city's only remaining Georgian square.

E) Slippery Road sign, a sign said to be associated with a roller coaster called Russian Mountains that was located at that spot.

F) Empty paint tubes, the Royal Society of Artists Gallery is near by.

G) Rubber teats, St Paul's Square was a popular promenading spot for Victorian nannies, which became known as 'Tittie bottle park'.

H) An Inkwell, outside Baker & Finnemore, famous manufacturers of pen nibs.

I) Borax, used in jewellery making to produce a flux for soldering.

J) Casting tree, used to produce multiple objects.

K) Building bricks, the brick building is the School of Jewellery, over a century old.

L) Flag, the Victoria Works used for pen making was, apparently, also known as Flag House.

M) Signatures, the nearby Victoria Works received many visitors who viewed pen-making techniques and they signed a visitors' book.

You can then cross over the road and complete the return journey looking out for:

N) Running man, couriers running from place to place.

O) Steel bangle, worn by Sikhs at the Gurdwara Temple.

P) Farthings, the mint was not far from this spot where coinage was made for countries all over the globe.

Q) Buses, the building was the headquarters of West Midlands Travel.

R) Curb chain, symbolising one of the many activities of the area, chain making.

S) Gold chocolate bar commemorating the chocolate manufacturer Cadbury's and the jewellery trade.

T) Taps, these are near to the offices of Severn Trent Water Authority.

U) Bench peg, a tool of the trade.

V) Plated sample, outside the factory where electroplating was invented.

W) Film projector, the now-demolished factory on the site invented celluloid used to make film.

X) Heart with canal, canals were used to transport jewellery and the raw goods needed to manufacture it.

Y) Stamp letter, used to stamp jewellery.

Z) Telephone receiver, BT tower is nearby.

MOTOR CITY: BRRRUUUMMM!

Herbert Austin set up his car business in Longbridge. He lived in Australia as a youngster, and was involved in the Wolseley Sheep Shearing Company.

Back home by 1895 he set up his car business and his Austin 7 became a must-have and in 1922 they were selling for over £200.

In more modern times the first Metro car rolled off the production line at Longbridge in October 1980 and over 4,000 were sold in the first two weeks.

In its first full month, November 1980, 7,000 Metros were sold, making it the second biggest seller behind the Ford Cortina.

Metro sales reached 500,000 within three years.

The millionth Metro came off the production line in October 1986.

Austin Rover closed in April 2005 and more than 6,000 workers were thrown onto the dole queue following the collapse into administration of the firm.

In April 2011 the Shanghai Automotive Industry Corporation began production again at Longbridge. The MG6 is the first new model MG to be mass-produced in the UK for 16 years. Most of the vehicle is made in China but assembled at Longbridge.

Longbridge's only female factory worker (at the time), Lisa Ponter, drove the first car off the production line. 400 people are working at Longbridge in design, engineering and assembly roles.

11

SPORT

FOOTBALL

There are two professional clubs in Birmingham, Birmingham City and Aston Villa. A third club, West Bromwich Albion are just over the political boundary in Sandwell, although until boundary reorganisation in 1974 part of the ground was in Birmingham.

In 1888, William McGregor of Aston Villa FC invited other clubs to play regularised games of football, leading to the creation of the Football League.

Aston Villa and West Bromwich Albion were two of the original twelve members of first Football League Championship in 1888/9.

West Bromwich Albion would have been the very first table-toppers. Albion won 2–0 at Stoke in front of 4,500 spectators and would have headed Preston North End, Derby County and Everton by virtue of goal average, but no table was produced for this first game. West Brom went on to finish sixth in the table.

In April 2011 it was revealed that Birmingham has produced the third highest number of players to play in the Prmier League of any English city with 56 of the 1,323 footballers who have played in the Premiership since its inception in 1992 being born in Birmingham.

BIRMINGHAM CITY'S FOUR NAMES

Birmingham City Football Club was formed in 1875 by a group of Holy Trinity Cricket Club players who wanted to do something during the winter months. Here are the four names they've had over their history.

1875   Small Heath Alliance
1888   Small Heath
1905   Birmingham
1943   Birmingham City

BIRMINGHAM CITY'S FOUR GROUNDS

Arthur Street, Bordesley Green
Ladypool Road, Sparkbrook
Muntz Street, Small Heath
St Andrew's, Small Heath

Muntz Street was a field rented for an initial £5 a year from the family of Sam Gressey.

Two years later, they paid £90 to Aston Villa for a stand from Villa's former ground in Perry Barr. The club transported it piece by piece, and re-erected it as a terrace cover behind the goal at the Muntz Street end.

The first game at Muntz Street, a friendly match against Saltley College, was played on 11 September 1877. Small Heath Alliance won 5–0, in front of a crowd that generated gate receipts of 6s 8d.

The last game at Muntz Street was played on 22 December 1906. Birmingham beat Bury 3–1. The last goal was scored by Arthur Mounteney.

St Andrew's has been their home ground since 1906. It was described as, 'a wilderness of stagnant water and muddy slopes'.

Tradition has it that gypsies, evicted from the site before work could begin, laid a 100-year curse on the club.

To create height for the terracing on the Coventry Road side of the ground, the club offered the site as a tip, local people paying a total of £800 for dumping an estimated 100,000 loads of rubbish. That stand was demolished in 1994 and it was said that it cost £250,000 to decontaminate the land.

St Andrew's was officially opened by Sir John Holder on 26 December 1906, when Birmingham played out a 0–0 draw with Middlesbrough in a First Division fixture. There had been heavy snowfall overnight, and dozens of volunteers, including members of the club's board, worked all morning to clear the pitch. The game finally kicked off an hour late.

Benny Green scored the first goal at St Andrew's on 29 December 1906, three days after the official opening. Benny was rewarded with a piano. He later played for Burnley, Preston and Blackpool before joining the King's Own Royal Lancaster Regiment and was killed in action at Arras on 26 April 1917. His name is on the Arras War Memorial.

The club supported the war effort by allowing the ground to be used as a rifle range for military training during the First World War.

During the Second World War the main stand, which was being used as a temporary fire station, burned down, destroying the club's records, when a fireman mistook a bucket of petrol for water when intending to damp down a brazier.

QUIRKY, BUT INTERESTING, BIRMINGHAM CITY FACTS

The Blues made their first trip to Wembley in 1931, but, sadly for them, they were beaten 2–1 in the FA Cup final by rivals West Bromwich Albion.

Birmingham City played in the 1956 FA Cup final against Manchester City when Bert Trautmann, Manchester City's goalkeeper, suffered a broken neck – the Blues still lost.

Birmingham City didn't win a major trophy until the League Cup in 1963 when they beat rivals Aston Villa 3–1 on aggregate. It took them forty-eight years to win their next major trophy when in February 2011 they won the competition for the second time, under its new name of the Carling Cup, beating the media's favourites Arsenal 2–1.

Joe Bradford is the club's all-time record goalscorer with 267 goals in 445 appearances.

Birmingham, then Small Heath, won 12–0 against Walsall Town Swifts on 17 December 1892, a record number of goals scored by the Blues, which was equalled in 1903 but has never been beaten.

On the opening home game of the season on 13 September 1902 the Blues beat Manchester City 4–0 to start a sequence which saw them unbeaten at home all season, with 17 consecutive wins. They finished second in the league behind Manchester City. The sequence included a 12–0 win over Doncaster Rovers on 11 April 1903 to record the joint highest number of goals scored in a match.

There is some confusion over the attendance record, it is either 66,844 or 67,341, and was set at a 1939 FA Cup tie against Everton.

The highest attendance recorded for a league match is 60,250, against Aston Villa in the First Division on 23 November 1935.

Trevor Francis made his full debut for Birmingham against Cardiff at Ninian Park in September 1970, aged just sixteen. The highlight of his first season came on 20 February 1971, when he scored all four goals in a win over Bolton at St Andrew's, becoming the first ever sixteen-year-old to achieve this feat in league football. He later became England's first £1 million player when he left to join Nottingham Forest.

Robert Firth, born in Sheldon in February 1887 played for Birmingham Corporation Transport, before joining Birmingham, then known as Small Heath. Later in his career he coached Real Madrid for two years, 1932–4, where he won the La Liga title. His only honour in England appears to be winnning the North Staffordshire Infirmary Cup in 1922 while with Port Vale.

The current Birmingham City Football club logo features a ball and a globe and was designed by Michael Wood, a fan who won a design competition run by the *Sports Argus*. The new logo was revealed in the matchday programme on 25 March 1972.

Birmingham didn't play in the 1920/1 FA Cup because they forgot to send the registration form in.

St Andrew's played host to the South African touring rugby union team which beat a Midland Counties XV 16–5 in December 1960.

At St Andrew's in June 1949, Dick Turpin beat Albert Finch on points to retain his British and Empire middleweight boxing title. The referee was called Ben Green, the namesake of the man who scored the first goal at the ground.

On 15 June 1965, Henry Cooper defeated Johnny Prescott at St Andrew's to retain his British and Empire heavyweight title; the fight took place two days after originally scheduled, having been rained off.

Birmingham City's players may have kicked off the 2010/11 season wearing their new strip but none of their fans did. Production of the kit was held up in China, owner Carson Yeung's homeland, due to the horrendous floods that devastated vast areas of the country.

ASTON VILLA HIGHS & LOWS

Biggest win: 13–0 v Wednesbury, FA Cup, October 1886
Biggest defeat: 1–8 v Blackburn Rovers, FA Cup, 3 February 1889
Top league scorer in a season: Pongo Waring, 49 goals, 1930/1
Highest goalscorer: Harry Hampton, 215, 1904–1915
Most capped player: Paul McGrath 80 caps for Republic of Ireland
Most league appearances: Charlie Aitken 561, 1961–76. He spent the last two seasons of his professional career in the NASL with the New York Cosmos.
Record home attendance: 76,588 v Derby County, FA Cup sixth round in March 1946.

When Andy Gray left Villa and signed for Wolves on 8 September 1979 for £1,469,000, he became the most expensive footballer in Britain.

Arthur Brown played for Villa in the 1880s. He was their first international player, making three appearances for England in 1882 and he scored four goals.

The highest attendance in the all-seater era was 42,788 which was recorded on 29 December 2009 in a Premiership game against Liverpool.

The record fee for a player paid is £18 million (rising to £24 million) to Sunderland for Darren Bent on 18 January 2011.

VILLA & THE 1966 WORLD CUP

Villa Park staged three games as part of the 1966 World Cup finals:

Spain v Argentina
Argentina v West Germany
West Germany v Spain

VILLA PARK & EURO '96

When England hosted Euro '96, Villa Park was chosen to host four games.

Holland 0–0 Scotland (34,363)
Holland 2–0 Switzerland (36,800)
Scotland 1–0 Switzerland (34,926)
Czech Rep 1–0 Portugal, quarter-final (26,832)

Record match receipts £1,196,712: Portugal v Czech Republic 23 June 1996.

GROUNDS FOR AMUSEMENT

Villa Park was built on the site of the Aston Lower Grounds Amusement Park, a 31¼-acre development that was opened to the public in 1872.

Flowers & Co., a brewery from Stratford-upon-Avon, owned it. They still owned the ground for the first few years after Villa moved in. It contained flowerbeds, sports pitches, pools, a bowling green, an aviary, a cycling track and a theatre.

In 1883 the grounds hosted lacrosse games played by Iroquois Indians from Canada.

England played a touring Australian cricket side there.

Villa moved on to the site in about 1897 when Dovehouse Pool was drained, filled in and became the pitch!

The club negotiated a twenty-one-year lease at a rental of £250 per year with an option of purchasing the land at 5s a square yard.

The first match to be played was a friendly against Blackburn Rovers on Easter Saturday, 17 April 1897. Villa won 3–0.

By 1911 the club had bought the adjoining carriage drive and bowling green and the old aquarium, skating rink and restaurant were used as offices.

The Witton Lane Stand was erected on the site of a sub-tropical garden.

Until 1914 there was a cycle track around the edge of the pitch.

During the Second World War the Trinity Road Stand was used as an air raid shelter and a rifle company occupied the home dressing room.

QUIRKY VILLA FACTS

Gershom Cox, born in Birmingham, was a full-back from 1888 to 1893. He scored the first goal in the Football League on the first day of the inaugural season, on 8 September 1888 while playing for Aston Villa against Wolves. Unfortunately, his goal was scored into his own net, thereby going into the record books for also scoring the first own goal.

In March 1975 Ron Saunders became the first manager to lead three different clubs to the League Cup final when Villa beat Norwich City 1–0.

Peter Aldis played in 294 games and went into the record books after he scored his only goal of his Aston Villa career against Sunderland, a header from 35 yards, which was a world record distance at the time.

On 27 February 1999, fourteen Englishmen appeared for Villa in their local derby with Coventry. No Premier League manager has since fielded an all-English starting XI.

Ted Drake holds the record for the most goals scored in a top flight game in English football, scoring seven against Aston Villa on 14 December 1935. 60, 891 people were there to see it.

In November 1923 Aston Villa player Tommy Ball was shot dead in his own garden by his next door neighbour, the only British professional footballer to be murdered. An argument blew up over Ball keeping a dog and chickens in his garden and George Stagg fired a fatal shot. He was convicted of murder but the Home Office decided to sanction life imprisonment rather than the death penalty. He was later declared insane and he died in 1966 in a Birmingham mental home. A memorial to Ball stands in the grounds of St John's Church, Perry Barr.

Charlie Athersmith scored the fastest goal scored at Villa Park after just 9 seconds against Charlton Atheltic in December 1938.

Villa once started a game on 26 November and didn't finish it until 13 March. It happened in 1898/9 at Sheffield Wednesday. The game was abandoned after 79½ minutes because of bad light and the FA ordered the other 10½ minutes should be played, but it couldn't be fitted in until March. At the eventual completion Wednesday scored again and won 4–1.

Harry Parkes was born in Erdington and missed only twelve league games in seven seasons from 1947 to 1954. He became a successful sports shop owner with a shop in Erdington and more famously in the city centre at Corporation Street.

It is said that Villa star Steve Smith was signed in 1893 at the coalface when the club secretary went underground to get him to sign for them at the Cannock & Rugeley Colliery.

Albert Allen, who was born in Aston, played as an inside-forward for Villa. He made one appearance for England on 7 April 1888 when he scored three goals in a 5–1 victory over Ireland, thus making him one of only five England players to score a hat-trick on his only international appearance.

Villa fan Ian Lavender of *Dad's Army* fame played Private Pike and he always wore a scarf in Villa's colours of claret and blue.

Villa Park was the first English ground to stage England's international games in three different centuries. The first was in 1899, England 2–1 Scotland, while the first in the twentieth century was in 1902, England drawing 2–2 with Scotland. In the twenty-first century the ground hosted England 3–0 Spain in 2001.

Thirty-nine-year-old goalkeeper Brad Friedel became Villa's oldest player with his appearance in the 3–1 defeat to Manchester United in February 2011.

HOW VILLA WON & LOST THE FA CUP IN THE SAME YEAR!

Aston Villa won and lost the FA Cup in 1895! The team beat West Bromwich Albion 1–0 in that year's FA Cup final at Crystal Palace. Bob Chatt scored the goal after just 30 seconds, a record for the quickest cup final goal at the time. On night of 11/12 September 1895 the FA Cup was stolen from the shop window of William Shillcock, football and football boot manufacturer, of Newtown Row, where it had been on display and it was never seen again. Aston Villa was fined £25, a sum which paid for the new trophy provided by Vaughton's Ltd of the Jewellery Quarter.

SEVEN NON-FOOTBALL EVENTS HELD AT VILLA PARK

Local band Duran Duran played a concert in 1983. 18,000 people turned up and money raised went to MENCAP.

The American evangelist Billy Graham attracted 257,181 people to a series of prayer meetings in 1984.

Archbishop Desmond Tutu held a religious gathering at the stadium in 1989.

A Bruce Springsteen concert in June 1988 attracted 40,000 fans.

There was an England v Australia rugby international in 1947 with possibly the quickest try ever scored in Britain, the Australian captain scoring within 13 seconds.

On 21 June 1972 Danny McAlinden defeated Jack Bodell in a British and Empire lightweight title fight.

The first ever American football 'Summerbowl' in 1985 was played between the London Ravens and the Streatham Olympians.

CELEBRITY VILLA FANS INCLUDE . . .

Nigel Kennedy, violinist
Floella Benjamin, children's TV presenter
John Taylor, musician with Duran Duran
Jane Sixsmith, former England Ladies hockey player
Sir Norman Fowler, former MP and Chairman of the Conservative
   Party
Tom Hanks, actor
Prince Harry
David Cameron

A CANTER THROUGH HORSE RACING HISTORY

Birmingham had a number of small racecourses but none of them stood 'furlong' except for the one at Bromford Bridge, which became the number one venue in Brum for racing enthusiasts. There was mounting excitement, at least for the jockeys, when the first race was held. Philology ridden by Fred Finlay won that first race on 14 June 1895. Sadly, pressures on the land led to the whole site being sold to the council for housing. 1,900 homes for 7,500 people were built on the 180-acre site.

Welshman, ridden by Greville Starkey, won the last race, the appropriately named Farewell Maiden Plate, on 21 June 1965. Plantation Inn finished last and is therefore saddled with the dubious honour of being known as the last horse ever to cross the finishing line at Bromford Bridge. Around 9,000 spectators turned out that evening – nearly twice the average attendance.

The closure was a sad day for Francis Ford, who had been Clerk of the Course since 1953. His grandfather W.J. Ford and his uncle William had opened the course in 1895. The main stand was taken to Hednesford Hills Raceway stock car racing circuit. The winning post survives to this day, it is in a children's playground on Bromford Drive. People who moved into the new houses on the site found themselves with addresses named after horses. These include: Arkle Croft, Reynoldstown Road and Tulyar Croft.

STREETS BUILT ON BROMFORD BRIDGE WHICH WERE NAMED AFTER RACECOURSES

Cheltenham Drive
Folkestone Croft
Haydock Close
Kempton Park Road
Redcar Croft
Stratford Walk
Tipperary Close
Warwick Close
Wincanton Croft

Doncaster Way
Goodwood Close
Hexham Croft
Newmarket Way
Sandown Road
Thirsk Croft
Towcester Croft
Wetherby Close
York Drive

FIVE STREETS BUILT ON BROMFORD BRIDGE THAT WERE NAMED AFTER DERBY WINNERS

Papryus (1923)
Trigo (1929)
Hyperion (1933)
Tulyar (1952)
Pinza (1953)

FIVE STREETS BUILT ON BROMFORD BRIDGE THAT WERE NAMED AFTER GRAND NATIONAL WINNERS

Reynoldstown (1935 & 1936)
Sprig (1927)
Sundew (1957)
Kilmore (1962)
Ayala (1963)

HORSE-ING AROUND BRUM

A racehorse named Birmingham was stabled in Sherlock Street, on a spot now occupied by the wholesale markets. The gee-gee now makes a good pub quiz question, as it went on to win the St Leger in 1830, the oldest of Britain's classic five races. Its jockey was Patrick Conolly, who that year had also won the 2,000 Guineas on Augustus.

FACTS ABOUT THE NATIONAL INDOOR ARENA

Architects Hellmuth, Obata & Kassabaum of Kansas City designed it.

Linford Christie officially opened the NIA on 4 October 1991.

The huge frame structure spans 130 metres by 90 metres creating a column-free interior.

The main arena bowl is 100 metres long and 60 metres wide.

It houses Britain's first demountable six-lane, 200-metre athletics track.

It contains up to 8,000 fixed seats, 4,000 retractable seats and additional flat floor seating.

It was built over the main Birmingham to Wolverhampton railway line meaning trains called 'Sprinters' run beneath the sprinters in a 125 metre long by 11 metre high tunnel.

There is a community hall measuring 72 metres in length.

Liz McColgan and Noureddine Morceli broke two world records at the first international athletics meeting held at the NIA, the TSB International.

The ITV programme *Gladiators* was filmed at the NIA.

THE NIA OPENING FESTIVAL OF SPORT

The opening Festival of Sport featured:

Friday 4 October 1991: The opening ceremony and the Birmingham Classic Gymnastics event.

Saturday 5 October 1991: Trampoline World Cup and the American All-Stars v England basketball.

Sunday 6 October 1991: National Fitness Festival and England v Canada netball.

Monday 7 October 1991: the Mars Olympic Torch relay and England v Japan badminton.

Tuesday 8 October 1991: The World Wrestling Federation European Rampage.

After that the NIA showed its versatility by staging Verdi's opéra *Aida* with a cast of 600 . . . then there was the portable ice mat for Disney on Ice.

THE BIRMINGHAM SUPERPRIX

The Birmingham Superprix were held in August 1986, 1987, 1988, 1989 and 1990.

The first event was held on 24 and 25 August 1986 with the main race being the Halford's Superprix Round 9 of the FIA International Formula 3,000 Championship.

The first Superprix winner was Luis Peréz-Sala.

It was raced over 52 laps of a 2.47-mile circuit on five roads in the city centre.

Cars reached speeds of up to 160mph.

70,000 people turned up to watch it, presumably meaning 140,000 earplugs were distributed!

8 miles of Armco steel crash barriers surrounded the circuit.

OTHER SPORTING SNIPPETS

Mark Lewis-Francis of Birchfield Harriers ran the anchor leg in the 4×100m relay team, at the 2004 Athens Olympic games. The GB team took gold, making him the youngest British Athletics Olympic champion since 1936.

Denise Lewis won the gold medal for the heptathlon at the 2000 Sydney Olympics. She won a bronze medal at the 1996 Olympics. Her personal best points score of 6,831 points remains the highest score by a GB athlete and it is a Commonwealth record.

In 2007 Boxer Frankie Gavin became English boxing's first ever World Amateur champion.

Rugby star Sam Doble was born in Wolverhampton but worked in Birmingham as a PE teacher at Northfield Comprehensive School. He played 330 first team games for Moseley scoring over 3,000 points. He was capped three times for England and scored 24 points in England's historic 18–9 victory over South Africa in 1972.

The World Table Tennis Championships were held at the NEC in 1978. A 20ft service throw by the Chinese caught everyone's attention and was later banned.

William Snook of Birchfield Harriers was the first amateur athlete to get a life ban from the sport by the AAA. In 1896 he came second in a race but was suspended for life for 'not trying to win'. It was claimed he was in league with bookmakers and was under orders not to finish first. He claimed he had blistered feet, but the ban stood.

Lawn tennis originated on the lawn of a house in Birmingham, the home of Major T.H. Gem, a solicitor. Major Gem's opponent that day was J. Perera, and they devised the rules that still stand today. The house, in Ampton Road, still stands and is called Fairlawns.

The Edgbaston Archery and Lawn Tennis Society is the oldest surviving lawn tennis club in the world.

The Edgbaston Priory Tennis Club, the venue for the DFS Challenge, has hosted five Davis Cup tennis tournaments.

Ann Jones MBE, the winner of the Ladies Singles title at Wimbledon in 1969, beat Billy Jean King. Her father Adrian Haydon was England's table tennis captain and played cricket for Kings Heath. Her mother also played table tennis for England.

'The Tennis Girl' shows a young woman from behind walking towards the net of a tennis court with a tennis racquet in her right hand and her left hand reaching behind lifting her short tennis dress, showing she is not wearing any underwear. The photograph was taken by Martin Elliott in September 1976 and features eighteen-year-old Fiona Butler, his girlfriend at the time. The photograph was taken at Birmingham University and the poster was first published as part of a calendar by Athena in 1977 and has sold over 2 million copies.

Slippery Sam was the name given to a Triumph bike, which won five successive TT races on the Isle of Man, but which was destroyed in a fire at the National Motorcycle Museum in 2003.

Mary, Ian and Peter Stewart were world-class athletes from the city. Mary was Commonwealth gold medallist and once held the indoor mile record holder. Peter won 5,000 metres gold at the Commonwealth Games in 1970 and Peter became the European Indoor champion and mile record holder.

The Birmingham & District Works Amateur Football Association was once the largest in the world. At the outbreak of the Second World War there were 278 teams in the association.

The Birmingham Angling Association is the largest association in the country with at least 200 clubs and 10,000 members. It had a membership of nearly 70,000 anglers with 1,200 affiliated clubs when at its peak in the mid-1970s.

Nigel Mansell was the 1992 Formula One motor racing world champion. He was born in Upton upon Severn in 1953, but spent much of his time in Birmingham and was described by *The Times* as 'Birmingham's fastest son'.

Ian Emes from Handsworth is a British animator who has worked with musicians Pink Floyd. However, Emes' father, Ronald, was a Birmingham policeman who trained the British canoe team at four Olympic Games.

Cricket was first mentioned in Birmingham in the mid-eighteenth century when the landlord of the Bell Inn, adjacent to the present-day Smallbrook Queensway, advertised for matches for his team.

Warwickshire County Cricket Club was formed on 8 April 1882 in the Regent Hotel, Leamington, at the suggestion of William Ansell

– the schoolmaster had previously been responsible for the formation of the Birmingham Association of Cricket Clubs.

Alastair Cook hit 294, the highest individual score at the Edgbaston ground, as England beat India in August 2011. His 803-minute innings is the longest by any batsman.

Warwickshire have won the County Championship on six occasions: 1911, 1951, 1972, 1994, 1995 and 2004.

In July 1997 Edgbaston was the scene of the first competitive floodlit day-night cricket match in Britain.

In May 1902 Edgbaston Cricket Ground, Birmingham's oldest international sports venue, staged its first Test match when Australia were bowled out for 36 runs! England were 376 for 9 when they declared. John Thomas Tyldesley hit 136 for England, but the match was ultimately drawn.

The Belfry Golf Course has hosted the Ryder Cup on four occasions; Europe won three times and one tournament was drawn.

Birmingham lost out to Barcelona in the race to win the Olympic Games of 1992. The decision was announced at the International Olympic Committee meeting in Lausanne, Switzerland. Birmingham's Olympic bid President was Denis Howell MP.

Birmingham's hopes of staging the 1996 Olympics were shattered when Manchester won the British nomination in May 1988, but it was announced that Birmingham would hold the International Olympic Committee meeting at the new International Convention Centre in June 1991.

The June 1991 IOC meeting was opened by the queen on the day she opened the ICC, quite convenient really as it happened to be in the very same building that she just had declared open.

In August 1995 Birmingham unveiled plans for an 85,000-seater national stadium that, if it had been built, would have cost £202 million. The city hoped it would get support because of its central location. 27 million people lived within two hours of the proposed venue near the National Exhibition Centre. After really careful consideration, the powers that be chose to build our new national stadium in a difficult inaccessible part of the capital called Wemberleee.

Boxer Johnny Prescott grew up in an orphanage from the age of three after his mother died in an air raid and his father was killed on the beaches at Dunkirk. He went on to win his first 22 fights. His most famous fight was against Henry Cooper at Villa Park in 1965, he had to retire with an eye injury in the tenth round.

TEN BRUMMIE SPORTSMEN IN LESS WELL-KNOWN SPORTS

Keith Arkell, British chess champion in 2008, lived at Rednal, but probably not in a castle.

Pat Roach, wrestler turned actor and star of *Auf Wiedersehen, Pet*, grunted and groaned in Ladywood.

Visanthe Shiancoe, American footballer for the Minnesota Vikings, was born in Birmingham in June 1980, that's our Birmingham, not Birmingham, USA.

Andrew Symonds, an Australian all-rounder, was born in Birmingham in 1975, but moved to Oz as an adopted child when he was three months old. He could have played for England but opted for Australia and he made his Test debut in 1998. He holds the world record for hitting the most sixes in a first-class innings, 16, and once hit 254 runs in one innings.

Wilf O'Reilly won two speed skating gold medals at the 1988 Winter Olympics in Calgary, Canada.

Kenny Andrews, motorcycle sidecar racer, won the 1979 Scottish Sidecar Championship.

Bob Brettle, bare knuckle boxer, was born in Scotland but was known as 'The Birmingham Pet'. He is buried in St Peter's churchyard, Harborne.

Bernard Ford, former world and Olympic coach/choreographer and four-time British, European and World Ice Dance champion and World Professional Ice Dance champion is from Birmingham.

Harry Fowler won the twin-cylinder class of the 1907 Isle of Man TT Race .

Brummie John Curry, figure skater, won Britain's first Olympic gold medal in the sport in front of 10,000 people in Innsbruck. *The Times* called it, 'masterly in its cool beauty of movement'.

POT BLACK WINNERS

Pot Black was a BBC Birmingham production from Pebble Mill that made snooker a TV sport. It was a production to signal the introduction of colour television in 1969. It ran from 1969 until 1986 and was reintroduced for a few years from 1991 to 1993 and 2005 to 2007. Ray Reardon was the first winner of the tournament. Other winners were:

John Spencer
Graham Miles
Doug Mountjoy
Steve Davis
Jimmy White
Matthew Stevens
Ken Doherty

Eddie Charlton
Perrie Mans
Cliff Thorburn
Terry Griffiths
Neal Foulds
Mark Williams

12

AND ANOTHER THING . . .

OOOOPS . . . !

Warwickshire cricket captain Ashley Giles ordered mugs for his testimonial year. Unfortunately the prototype had the words 'King of Spain' rather than 'King of Spin' written on them. The error received much publicity and 200 were ordered by the club and soon sold out. The marketing men were no mugs!

In 2008 Birmingham City Council sent out about 720,000 pamphlets praising Brummies for recycling, at a cost of £15,000. The leaflet showed a photograph of the Birmingham skyline, but instead of showing landmarks such as the Rotunda and the new Selfridges building, it showed downtown Birmingham, Alabama, instead.

There are not five roads that meet at the traffic island at Five Ways, but there are six! When it was first called Five Ways there were five but when sixth was added the name wasn't changed.

When the Five Ways island was reconstructed in 1971 the ceiling on the underpass was a bit too low. The headroom was 16ft 5¾in – ¼in below the regulation 16ft 6in, so the tarmac was skimmed!

On 23 October 1933 the 40,000th council house in Birmingham was opened at 30 Hopstone Road, Weoley Castle, by Neville Chamberlain, the then Chancellor of the Exchequer. The newly painted front door stuck and Chamberlain had to wait while the keyhole was examined and the door was finally given a big push!

The Robin Hood Island at Hall Green, sadly, has nothing to do with robbing the rich to give to the poor. It seems the area was once known as 'Robin's Wood', but a mapmaker in the eighteenth century misspelt the name as 'Robin's Hood', and the name still stands today.

The equestrian statue of George I outside the Barber Institute at Birmingham University was purchased from Dublin Corporation. 'The king's left leg became detached from the statue just before its removal from Dublin', but was reaffixed in Brum.

Greece ordered 14 million 50 lepta coins in 1922 from the Birmingham Mint, but these coins never went into circulation because by the time they reached Greece the value of the metal was in excess of the face value of the coins.

In January 2008 the site of the last public hanging in Birmingham was marked with a plaque, after the spot was wrongly identified for a number of years. Philip Matsell was hanged in front of a crowd of 40,000 in August 1806 for shooting and wounding a peace officer, an early form of police officer. The execution took place on the corner of Great Charles Street and Snow Hill, not Ludgate Hill as first thought. The mix up may be because hangings in London took place in Ludgate Hill.

In February 1989 when the Hyatt Hotel bridge link was put in across Broad Street joining the hotel to the International Convention Centre there was controversy when it was believed the bridge was too short, a problem created when the original shape of the hotel was changed – apparently after the bridge was designed.

On 11 October 1967 Prime Minister Harold Wilson sued pop group The Move over a nude caricature on a postcard promoting their hit record 'Flowers in the Rain'. The Birmingham group made an apology in the High Court for a 'violent and malicious personal attack'.

No one could decide what logo the town should have on its hallmarked goods at the time that Birmingham got its own Assay Office. Delegations from Birmingham and Sheffield stayed at the Crown & Anchor Hotel in the Strand while the Act of Parliament was being read in London. The two towns tossed a coin using the name of the hotel, and so Birmingham, the most landlocked town in the country, got an anchor logo which has been used ever since. Today Birmingham's assay office is the largest in the world, testing up to 80,000 items each working day.

On Easter Tuesday 1974 pop group Paper Lace used a derelict building opposite the Mint as a backdrop for the a photo shoot for their new album 'The Night Chicago Died', dressed as Chicago gangsters complete with imitation guns. A 999 call alerted police who promptly arrived at the scene. Mint security officials, later quoted in the works magazine *The Mint*, said 'the guns looked real from where we were and we kept them under surveillance until the police arrived.'

A statue of Sir Robert Peel stood in Victoria Square but was removed after an incident on 11 November 1926. The driver of a large lorry, who presumably failed to keep his eyes peeled, struck a gas lamp that fell across the statue and hit Peel on the head. The statue toppled onto the carriageway and was subsequently removed. Today he stands outside the police training centre at Tally Ho!

In 1991 the Birmingham Convention and Visitor Bureau complained to British Rail that passengers coming to Birmingham from London were getting off the train at Birmingham International station, 10 miles from the city centre's New Street station because they were confused by the name. They demanded New Street be renamed Birmingham Central or Birmingham City Centre station. The *Birmingham Post* stated: 'if Birmingham is to welcome its growing contingent of foreign visitors it should stop confusing them over the names of its two main railway stations,' and called for Birmingham International station to be renamed Birmingham Airport station. It wasn't.

Telly Savalas of *Kojak* fame heaped praise on the city when he did the voiceover for a public relations film that was shown in cinemas in the late 1970s. *Telly Savalas Looks at Birmingham* was a 25-minute colour film which featured Spaghetti Junction, the Balti belt and the Bullring. He said, 'It's my kinda town!' It was revealed that he had never visited Birmingham!

When Birmingham began flirting with tourism, the powers that be decided to spend £300,000 by bringing in consultants to devise a catchy slogan to be used in advertisements for the city. These were some of the printable suggestions:

Birminghambition
Up and Brumming

SECOND TO NONE

On 8 March 1957 the Minister of Transport created a bigger bang than expected when he started work on the new Inner Ring Road. The spectators were showered with debris when the explosive charge used to start construction was more powerful than anticipated. A press photographer had to be taken to hospital with a head injury, but I suppose the negative publicity wasn't too bad!

The new Minister of Transport, Ernest Marples, opened the first section of the Inner Ring Road on 11 March 1960. This section was only 400 yards long and had cost £1,160,000, which equals £2,900 per yard or £5,104,000 per mile! The final scheme cost around £33 million, the original estimate was £15 million.

In 1971 the queen officially opened the Ring Road. She was supposed to name a half-mile section of tunnel 'Queensway' and the rest was to be called 'Ringway', but she called the whole road 'Queensway' and so it was decided to call it by that name officially and road signs were changed.

A pub football side, the Royal George from Kingstanding, faced Barcelona in the Nou Camp in 1962. They were soundly beaten 15–1 but what an experience it must have been. They were playing in a youth tournament, the Easter Trophy, and beat Hamburg and Espanyol for the right to play Barca. Apparently the Spanish organisers thought they were Birmingham City when they first arrived but allowed them to continue when finding out who they really were.

BIRMINGHAM MAY BE ONE OF THE MOST LANDLOCKED CITIES, BUT . . .

Birmingham has a long association with raising and equipping lifeboats with around forty lifeboats being funded from collections made in Birmingham.

Chance Brothers glassworks of Smethwick, was a leading glass manufacturer under the direction of Robert Lucas Chance who lived in what is now Summerfield Park. He was joined by his brother William who owned a successful iron merchants in Great Charles Street. Together they became the largest British manufacturer of plate and optical glass, thus proving that many hands make light work! They focussed on their optical business and saw the light at the

end of the tunnel that led to the business expanding into lighthouse engineering. The brothers established a highly successful business that revolutionised lighthouse lenses. They had a bright future, off and on, off and on, off and on, for a number of years.

OTHER SEA STORIES THAT GO DOWN WELL

Vaughton's of Birmingham produced medals made of 9 carat gold. They were presented to crew members who survived the *Titanic* disaster.

It is thought that four Birmingham-born people were working on *Titanic* and all died, and there were four passengers with Birmingham connections, these included:

William Hipkins, managing director of Avery Scales who was actively looking for overseas markets. He set sail for USA on the *Titanic* from Southampton. His body, if found, was never identified. He lived in Augustus Road, Edgbaston. He was on a first-class ticket which cost £50.

Henry Samuel Morley, alias Mr Henry Marshall, a confectioner, aged thirty-eight, died.

Miss Kate Florence Phillips, alias Mrs Kate Marshall, survived. Kate Phillips gave birth to a daughter, Ellen Mary 'Betty', on 11 January 1913. It has been suggested that Miss Phillips was having an affair with Henry Morley, and the two were running away together. Morley perished, but Kate survived and gave birth to her daughter almost nine months to the day after the sinking. It is possible that Betty was conceived on board the *Titanic*.

ANIMAL MAGIC?

A squirrel appeared on the crest of the Holte family of Aston Hall. The creature was later used on the logo of Ansells brewery based not far from the hall.

Two dinosaurs made an appearance in Aston Park in July 1938. The near 15ft-high creatures were models used in the city's centenary pageant.

Chipper is a well-known cartoon dog with his own club in the *Birmingham Mail*. Cartoonist Len Pardoe drew the first cartoon in 1949; he passed away in 2002 aged seventy-nine. It was said he turned down the chance to become assistant to Frank Hampson, creator of Dan Dare in the *Eagle* comic to take upon his role at the *Birmingham Mail*.

For more than thirty-five years, local MP Percy Shurmer treated poverty-stricken children living in Birmingham to an annual Christmas party. They were known as the Little Sparrows.

Tingha and Tucker, two TV puppet koala bears, went along the 'Wibbly, Wobbly Way' between 1962 and 1970. They had friends such as Willie Wombat and Katie Kookaburra. Unlike their 'Boomerang Woomerang' they went away in 1970 and didn't return.

Dash, the Snow Hill station dog at the turn of the twentieth century, was depicted in the mosaic mural of the Great Western Railway in St Chad's Circus.

The comedy entertainer Bob Carolgees who appeared on the Saturday morning TV series *Tiswas* was best known for appearing with a puppet named Spit the Dog.

The bronze bull statue in the Bullring is 4.5 metres in length and weighs about 6.5 tonnes. It is one of the largest bronze animal sculptures in the country.

A wallaby was on show at the International Convention Centre in April 1991 for the 'soft' opening of the first convention, the International Veterinary Congress. It hopped around the mall entrance for the members of the press and christened the floor before leaping off into history.

A paw print of a black labrador called Ebony can be seen at the base of Queen Victoria's statue in Victoria Square. The dog was an unofficial watchdog during the renovation of the area in 1993. Her owner, Larry Dawe from Harborne, was a stonemason on the site.

Roy Rogers and his trusty steed Trigger visted the Hippodrome in 1954. A vast crowd of 5,000 besieged the old Queen's Hotel and Trigger, holding a pen between his teeth, signed the register!

Wild West legend Buffalo Bill and his horse trotted along New Street in June 1903 to promote his Wild West show.

In March 1930 when a big top circus at Spring Hill was destroyed by fire, Togare the lion tamer, made the headlines when he used raw eggs and olive oil to soothe the burns on the skin of the lions.

Lewis's department store was famous for its Pets' Corner. They had animals on display and some for sale. During the summer they had an outside display on the roof.

A dead cat was discovered beneath the flooring during restoration work at the former Curzon Street station and it is still on display there. It is believed it was customary to entomb live cats in buildings for superstitious reasons.

In 1858 Queen Victoria opened Aston Hall as a public museum. There was giraffe and rhinoceros in the entrance hall, both stuffed!

'Gladly' was the name of a bear kept at the Botanical Gardens in the early 1920s. It was named after a line in the hymn 'Gladly, my cross I'd bear'. He lived alongside Rupert the ram, Walter the wallaby, and Algy and Miss Issi the alligators.

A leaping deer is the traditional logo of brewers Mitchells & Butlers who joined forces in 1898. Walking across the open countryside between the two breweries on Broad Street and Cape Hill at Smethwick the owners often saw deer running around, and that was before they had been drinking! Part of the area near the Smethwick brewery became known as Deer's Leap. A leaping deer has appeared on signs and beermats ever since.

In March 1958 a Triceratops dinosaur arrived at the Birmingham Museum from the USA. It was only the third one to arrive in the UK and had been dug up in Hell Creek, Montana in 1908.

Babu, a red panda, made national news when he got out of his enclosure at Birmingham Nature Centre in Cannon Hill Park. Police, in their panda cars, searched for Babu, and he caused panda-monium, spending four days on the run before being recaptured. He made 'a death-defying escape from a glass walled pen after a meal of bamboo,' according to the national press; locally it was reported that Babu had jumped out from the top of a tree or even been blown out of a tree and over the wall! What really happened no one will ever know, but we do know Babu was reunited in November 2005 with his brother, Tensing. They were split up again in January 2008 when Babu was moved to Edinburgh where he mated with Jodie, and, presumably, everyone lived happily ever after.

WE'RE AN ECO-FRIENDLY LOT IN BRUM

Birmingham had the first ever urban allotments in the country during the second half of the eighteenth century. They were known as the 'Guinea gardens' and were run by private owners for landless townies. By 1925 the Allotments Act required authorities to have allotments in town planning applications.

Lighting in the Tudor-style Selly Manor came from burning rushes. Dried rushes were drawn through animal fat and placed in special holders before being burned from one end; a 2ft rush could provide light for three quarters of an hour. Held horizontally it provided twice the light but burnt for a shorter time. This gave rise to the expression 'burning the candle at both ends'.

Selly Manor also has a surviving example of a Solar Room, a room in which ladies spent evenings to take advantage of the light from the west.

Over fifty trees were planted around the city centre in the autumn of 1992. London Plane trees were planted into New Street and Corporation Street and the delivery van then branched off to deliver hornbeam, hazel, lime and plane trees at Victoria Square. Sadly, the trees were imported from a nursery in Hamburg, 'none of the required size and quality could be bought in the UK', ex-plane-ed a city official.

When the Gas Hall in Edmund Street reopened in 1993 as an exhibition centre, it benefited from a computer simulation of the main gallery which assessed solar gain, air distribution and heating and cooling demand profiles. Which is just as well as the first exhibition contained paintings valued at over £100 million and without sufficient air conditioning such exhibitions wouldn't be possible.

The International Convention Centre on Broad Street can be said to be to be the biggest greenhouse in Europe. Its climate-controlled temperature is ideal for the fig trees in the mall. The council purchased them for the large fig-ure of £350,000 from a nursery in the Netherlands in 1991.

The Fort Dunlop office block near Spaghetti Junction opened in 2006 and has the largest living grass roof in the country providing natural insulation and a wildlife reserve.

In 1868 thirty lime trees were planted along A roads. The first road to twig what was going on was Bristol Road, making it the first tree-trunk road, but it was reported that many died in a dry summer that followed.

Each year over 75,000 bedding plants and over 1,000 shrubs are planted in Victoria Square.

Birmingham has a blooming good record at the Chelsea Flower Show and National Britain in Bloom awards, winning 14 consecutive gold medals. In May 1996 Birmingham's record at Chelsea was mentioned in parliament, an Early Day Motion stating, 'That this House congratulates the City of Birmingham Parks Department on its Chelsea Flower Show gold medal award for its display of more than 15,000 flowers marking 100 years of motoring; this follows a gold medal award last year, bringing to 16 the number of gold medals achieved; and commends the display to judges of the Britain in Bloom Competition as the City's entry.'

In recent years the medals won at the Chelsea Flower Show have been created by the Jewellery Quarter-based company, Toye Kenning & Spencer.

The Energy Centre on the International Convention Centre canal side produces enough hot water to wash up after a 3,000-seat banquet. It can also produce 50 tonnes of ice per hour and it has the capacity to heat an equivalent of 700 houses. It provides energy for the ICC, National Indoor Arena and Hyatt Hotel.

The Birmingham Trees for Life group planted its first tree in 2006, since then it has branched out across the city and planted its 10,000th tree at Chinn Brook Meadow in March 2011.

THIS WAS A GREAT IDEA, BUT . . .

A £400 million plan to tunnel under the city centre to allow the Metro to go from Five Ways to the NEC was derailed on cost grounds in 1996.

1990 saw the launch of a plan to build a five-star hotel in the shape of the RMS *Mauretania*, a former Cunard liner, next to the National Exhibition Centre. Councillor Albert Bore, chairman of the Economic Development Committee said, 'you have to admit there is a certain inventiveness about the scheme'. The plan, unlike the real ship, sank without trace.

In the mid-1980s Birmingham had a plan to put a 200 metre-long ski slope on the Lickey Hills, the fact that we don't get much snow didn't matter, as plastic type sheeting would have been used instead. Support for the scheme went downhill rapidly after 2,000 local residents and visitors protested.

In the 1930s the council was busy buying land at the city centre end of Broad Street with a view to developing a large civic complex that would be the envy of the world. Architects from across Europe were invited to submit plans and the winning design came from Paris. Work more or less got underway with Baskerville House being erected, but a little difficulty overseas, between 1939 and 1945, somewhat curtailed the plan and due to financial pressures Baskerville House was the only part of the scheme to be built.

TWIN CITIES

Birmingham has six partner or sister cities. They are:

Chicago, USA
Frankfurt, Germany
Leipzig, Germany
Johannesburg, South Africa
Lyon, France
Milan, Italy

There is also a treaty of friendship between Birmingham and Mirpur in Azad Kashmir, Pakistan, from where about 90,000 Birmingham citizens originate.

BIRMINGHAMS AROUND THE WORLD

Australia
Birmingham Creek, Tasmania

Canada
Birmingham, Saskatchewan
Birmingham Bay, Somerset Island

Ireland
Birmingham Castle, Athenry, Galway
Birmingham Castle, Carbury, Kildare (the castles are possibly named after a branch of the de Bermingham family)
New Birmingham, Tipperary

New Zealand
Birmingham, Wellington, North Island

The Moon, yes, the Moon!
Crater no. 357 is called Birmingham and apparently it lies within a larger crater called Hell. Oh dear.

United States of America
Birmingham, Jefferson, Alabama
Birmingham Port, Jefferson, Alabama
Birmingham, Los Angeles, California
Birmingham, New Haven, Connecticut
Birmingham, Fulton, Georgia
Birmingham, Schuyler, Illinois
Birmingham, Miami, Indiana
Birmingham, Van Buren, Iowa
Birmingham, Jackson, Kansas
Birmingham, Marshall, Kentucky
Birmingham, Oakland, Michigan
Birmingham, Lee, Mississippi
Birmingham, Clay, Missouri
Birmingham, Burlington, New Jersey
Birmingham, Erie, Ohio
Birmingham, Guernsey, Ohio
Birmingham, Allegheny, Pennsylvania
Birmingham, Chester, Pennsylvania
Birmingham, Delaware, Pennsylvania (1)
Birmingham, Delaware, Pennsylvania (2)
Birmingham, Huntingdon, Pennsylvania
Birmingham, Snohomish, Washington

TWENTY THINGS YOU'LL HEAR A TRUE BRUMMIE SAY

'By the looks of him he couldn't stop a pig in an entry' – something
  you might say to a bow-legged man.
'Av yow bin inoculated with a gramophone needle?' – said to
  someone who talks too much.
'He's 'umming 'n' arring' – hesitating.
'Enny road up, arr kid' – in any case.
'Geerr up the dancers' – told to a child who has misbehaved, it means
  go up the stairs to your room.
'He's in his oil tot' – a person who is really happy and content with
  what he is doing. Like me at the moment!
'She's all kippers 'n' curtains' – people who lived in posher areas
  but were not much better off than poorer people even though they
  made out they were.
'I'll 'av a macky sun, droi woit woin, arfa bitta and pointa moild' –
  what you might order in a pub.

'I've gorra pine in me belly' – what you say to the doctor when you've an upset stomach.

'Her eyes are bigger than her belly' – someone who has eaten too much and their belly is full.

'I've bin all round the Wrekin' – someone takes five minutes to get to the point, or someone who has been on an unnecessarily long journey.

'Look at 'er, 'ers gorra bob on herself' – someone who thinks they are better than they are.

'They've gone an' done a moonlight flit' – a family that moved house suddenly to avoid the rent man or bailiff.

'It worn't me' – what kids say to their mom when they've done something wrong, meaning 'I didn't do it.'

'And yow needn't come round 'er with yer arse in ya hand' – said to someone, usually a child, who is in a mood or temper.

'I'm on a line with you' – telling someone you are angry with him or her.

'She's running around like a blue-arsed fly' – someone in a hurry.

'Yom goooin yampy' – someone who is acting strange.

'That's a nice name to goo to bed with' – a sarcastic way of noting someone with a posh name.

'He's as drunk as a bobhowler' – someone who is drunk and appears uncoordinated, like a bobhowler, or moth, at a light bulb.

TWENTY BRUMMIE WORDS

Ackchully – actually I think you'll find these interesting.

Backerapper – a loud firework such as a banger.

Balmpot – someone whose is a bit daft.

Babby – the youngest person in the family, even if they are getting on a bit.

Flea pit – old time cinema with bugs who got in without paying.

Flummuxed – Confused.

Gazunder – a chamber pot usually used at night to save you going outside to the loo. It was stored under the bed, 'goes under', and was pulled out at the appropriate time (hopefully!).

Gawping – the Brummie way of staring open-mouthed.

Moithered – when someone is over-concerned about something.

Narner – someone who has done something silly.

Necks wik – seven days' time.

Pitherin' – someone who is doing things that are aimless or filling time.

Saft – a daft person, as in 'Don't be saft'.

Scrage – a cut usually on the knee caused by rubbing along the ground.

Steelie – a kind of marble, often a ball-bearing. Not to be confused with a glarny or a gobbie.

Tarrarabit – goodbye.

Traipsin' – being dragged around the shops when you don't really want to.

Wassermarrer? – an expression asking someone what the matter is.

Wench – Or 'aar wench', a female.

Wess Middleuns – West Midlands.

Writ – Wrote, as in 'I writ it down'.

ACCENT ON

Actress Beryl Reid (1919–96), although born in Hereford, made a name for herself by playing Marlene in *Educating Archie*, where she had a thick Brummie accent – 'Moy noyme's Mar-leen.'

Brummie jokes, just murder the vowels and you will understand 'em!

What's the difference between a toy and a plaything?
You don't wear a plaything around your neck

What's the difference between the Rhine and the Amazon?
No one has ever written a song called 'Singing in the Amazon'.

How can you tell a whale from a dolphin?
A dolphin doesn't have spokes.

What's the difference between a buffalo and a bison?
You can't wash your hands in a buffalo.

What's the difference between an oak and a pine?
You don't go to the doctor with an oak.

Why is a toiler more useful than a labourer?
A toiler can put a roof over your head.

What's the difference between a gripe and a moan?
You can't eat a moan.

Other titles published by The History Press

Birmingham Then & Now

MARK NORTON

ISBN 978-0-7524-5722-2

Take a fascinating and nostalgic visual journey back to 1960s Birmingham to witness the much-loved Bullring and the streets and courts that were swept away during the last fifty years of development. Mark Norton presents many previously unpublis pictures alongside his own colour photographs of the area in th twenty-first century.

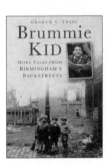

Brummie Kid

GRAHAM V. TWIST

ISBN 978-0-7524-5391-0

Brummie Kid is a fascinating recollection of the experience of growing up in the slums of Nechells and Aston. Despite hard liv conditions and a distinct lack of money, a strong community sp prevailed and families and neighbourhoods were close-knit. He are more funny, heart-warming stories from the backstreets of Birmingham which are sure to rekindle old memories.

Birmingham: A History in Ma

PAUL LESLIE LINE

ISBN 978-0-7524-6089-5

Accompanied with informative text and pic of the cityscape, the many detailed plans contained in this historic atlas of Birmingha are a gateway to its past, allowing the reade and researcher to visually observe the journe of this historic town to city status in 1889 a beyond.

Visit our website and discover thousands of other History Press books.

www.thehistorypress.co.uk